The Color Box

Language Themes Using Basic Teaching Strategies

Written by Anne Cotton & Fran Martin

Illustrated by Lyn Hope

D1449547

Published by
Teaching Resource Center
P.O. Box 82777
San Diego, CA 92138-9716

Printed in the United States of America
ISBN: 1-56785-011-1

Contents

Theme At A Glance

Trade Books & Big Books

A Rainbow Of My Own
Brown Bear, Brown Bear,
        What Do You See?
Freight Train
Johnny Appleseed
Listen To The Rain
Little Blue and Little Yellow
Rain
The Birthday Cake
The Snail's Spell

Crazy Color Creatures
I Am A Pirate
Ollie's Outing
Sing A Rainbow
The Birthday Cake
The Little Red House
To Town

Class Books & Booklets

Brown Tent In The Meadow Rewrite
Crayon Shaped Books
I Am A Cowboy
Ollie Saw...
Rhyme Time
To Town
Who Do You See?

Birthday Cake Buildup
Brown Bear
I Can Sing A Rainbow
Orange Is A Carrot
Rain
Red Is An Apple
The Little Red House
Yummy Sandwiches-
        Accordian Booklet

Songs

Colors- Hap Palmer
Crazy Color Creatures
Down By The Station
I Can Sing A Rainbow
Little Red Caboose
Orange Is A Carrot
Parade Of Colors - Hap Palmer

Rainstorm on Tape

Art

Apple Prints
Individual Freight Trains
Rain Bulletin Board
Rainbow Mobile
Sponge Paint Apple Tree
Who Do You See? Bulletin Board

Science & Math

Apple Activities - Math Their Way
Apple Graph
Blowing Bubbles
Create Rain - Experiment
Favorite Color Graph

Make Apple Sauce
Mixing Colors
Prism Rainbows
Snail Facts
Sort & Classify - Food & Transportation

Sort By Color

Drama

Brown Bear Stick Puppets
Little Blue And Little Yellow
Rainstorm on Tape
The Little Red House
The Snail's Spell
Vehicle Sounds - To Town

LYN

The Basic Teaching Strategies

In the development of this theme you will find phrases as **brainstorm for, develop in the pocket chart, sort and classify**, etc. To help clarify these phrases we have listed these basic teaching strategies and have given a brief description of each.

Fill with language:

This is when we read to the children. We read not only stories but poetry and factual information as well. We begin with a discussion of the illustrations to develop as much oral language as possible. We stop periodically to provide the opportunity for the child to anticipate and predict what might happen next. We also read a selection many times over to help make that selection become a part of the child. We feel strongly that we must continually *fill the child with language* as we move ahead with the theme.

Chanting:

Children need to work orally with the patterns of language. The primary way to do this with very young children is by chanting. This technique helps instill the rhythm and structure of language which then becomes a part of their everyday speech.

One way to chant is by using the my turn, your turn technique. The teacher reads a phrase and the children echo this phrase. The teacher tracks (runs hand under the text, pointing to each word) as the chanting takes place. Children may chant using the whole text (pictures, pictures and words, or words alone), or merely chant a repetitive phrase ("Not I," said the dog.) Chanting may be done using big books, charts, brainstorming ideas, pocket chart activities, trade books, etc. Songs and poems should also be included. When working with songs and poetry, we often add rhythmic hand movements which help instill the rhythm of the language and enhances the memorization.

Brainstorming:

Brainstorming is when children orally respond to a question posed by the teacher with the results usually being recorded where they may be seen by the children. This gives the teacher an insight into the children's knowledge. We usually begin a theme by brainstorming for what the children know about a given subject. A lack of ideas indicates that the children may need a *refill* of language and knowledge. The brainstorming is continuously being added to as the theme is developed.

Brainstorming is a whole class activity. The teacher begins by asking a question such as "What is green?" and elicits responses from the children. As the children respond, the teacher draws the appropriate pictures on the chalkboard and the children chant. **Note:** at the beginning of the kindergarten year, draw a picture only. No words are needed.

After the brainstorming, again chant all the pictures that were drawn: "A leaf is green. A turtle is green. Grass is green. A car is green." As the year progresses you will want to add words to the brainstorming:

Most brainstorming needs to be saved! As you work through a theme you will be continually referring to these ideas. Copy the brainstorming onto cards or chart paper. The cards may be displayed using masking tape, sticky side out. The chart may be used for matching and rebuilding. At a later date the chart may be cut apart and made into a strip book.

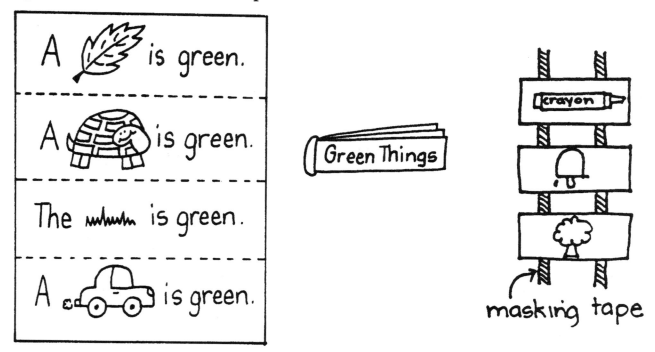

Another example of a brainstorming technique is to record ideas in categories that are not labeled. After the pattern is obvious, the children tell where to record the next idea. This method helps stimulate the children's thinking.

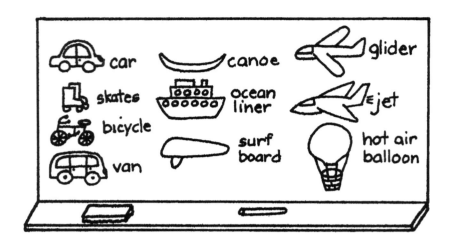

Sorting and Classifying:

 This when children look for likenesses and differences and put things together that are alike in some manner. The ideas from brainstorming activities are ideal for sorting and classifying. We usually begin classifying with groups of four to six children, with each group having about twenty cards or items to sort.

After this small group sorting activity, the whole class regroups and chants. Example: We classified according to color and then chanted, "A chair is green. An olive is green. A fat frog is green, etc." Gradually, we work toward activities that will involve individual classifications. The results of these activities may be graphed, producing either a real graph or a pictorial graph.[1]

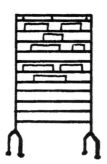

Develop in the Pocket Chart:

We use a pocket chart made of clear acetate and nylon.[2] You may use sentence strips or tagboard cards (laminated or contacted for a longer life) with the pocket chart. Whole texts, repeated phrases or pictures only may be used. There are a variety of ways to use the pocket chart. We listed our favorites:

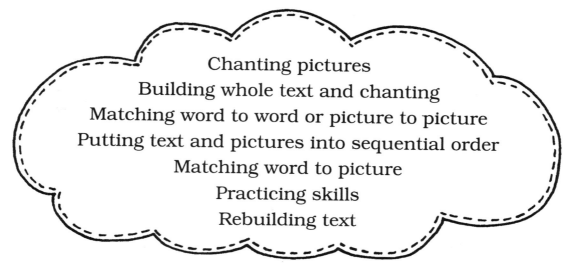

Chanting pictures
Building whole text and chanting
Matching word to word or picture to picture
Putting text and pictures into sequential order
Matching word to picture
Practicing skills
Rebuilding text

When we are developing a lesson in the pocket chart, we usually insert the appropriate pictures, or text and pictures, and then have the children chant **many** times. We may ask the children to hide their eyes and then we take something out of the text or merely turn it over.

The children then decide what is missing and chant to see if they are correct. We then take more than one word, picture, or phrase out (or turn them over) and repeat the process. The final task is to rebuild the entire text.

Samples:

Step 1:   Chanting pictures
            "A leaf is green."

Step 2: Build whole text and chant: "A leaf is green."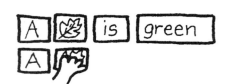

Step 3: Matching word to word or picture to picture: (Children match above, below, or on top of)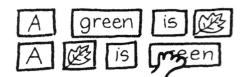

Step 4: Putting text and pictures into sequential order:

Step 5: Matching word to picture:

Step 6: Practicing skills:

- Find the word that says *green*.
- Find the word that says *is*.
- Find the word that comes before *green*.
- Find the word that comes after *is*.
- What sound do you hear at the beginning of the word *leaf*?

Step 7: Rebuilding: All pictures and text are distributed to the children and the complete story is built again in the pocket chart. Children read the text from the pocket chart, checking for accuracy.

Tracking:

 This involves moving your hand under and pointing to each word as it is read. This helps develop left to right progression as well as one-to-one correspon-

dence between the printed text and the spoken word.

Big Books:

These are enlarged versions of books, poems or songs. The print must be large enough so that it may be seen by the entire class. The enlarged print allows us to track as we read and helps to develop one-to-one correspondence. Many of the activities used with the pocket chart may also be used with big books. We laminate the pages of teacher-prepared big books and bind them with loose leaf rings. The rings may be taken out and the pages shuffled so that the children may sequence the big book. For obvious reasons **do not** number the pages. These books are really loved and used over and over by the children.

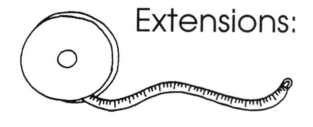

Extensions:

These are activities we practice what we learned during brainstorming, reading, chanting, and the various pocket chart activities. We try to incorporate the following:

Individual booklets: Each child makes his/her own booklet and should have the opportunity to read and track before taking it home.

Class book: Each child contributes a page and the book is kept in the classroom library.

Drama: Children act out the activity with **all** children taking **all** the parts. (a bit noisy but very effective)

Art: Children make illustrations for bulletin boards, booklets, plays, etc., using as many different kinds of art media as possible.

Make-a-play: Children retell a story by manipulating characters they have made.

Writing: All writing activities need to be extensively developed orally **first.**

1. Using a structure or frame, the children fill in the blanks by taking the ideas from the brainstorming activities.

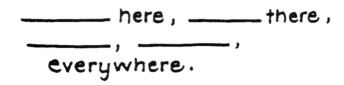

2. Creating innovations: children orally rewrite a familiar text using their own words. Example: (change "Brown bear, brown bear, what do you see?" to "Octopus, Octopus, what do you see?") This can be an individual or a whole group activity. The teacher may need to take dictation for the very young child.

3. Dictation: children individually illustrate and the teacher transcribes for them.

Draw with me: This is a whole class activity where language development is the goal. We do not consider this an art lesson. All the children are working with individual chalkboards at this time. We ask the children to name all the parts that need to be included to draw a specific object. A sample might be:

"What do we need to make a house?"

"A door"

"A roof"

"Windows"

(continue until entire picture is completed)

Individual sequencing: This is when each child puts pictures or a text into a specific order. This is usually a *cut and paste* activity. It varies in difficulty. We begin with pictures only, then pictures with the text, and finally the text alone. We also put the text in sequence with numerals, words, and pictures.

Pictures only:

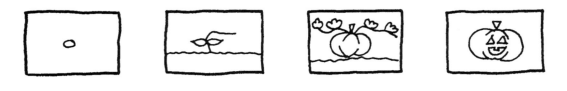

Pictures with text:

Numeral, text and picture:

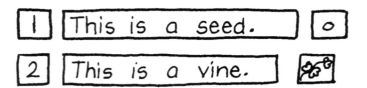

Homework: This is when we try to involve the family. The homework is occasional and we include a detailed explanation. This activity is returned to class and used for chanting, classifying booklet making or other language activities.

An example might be:

Dear Parents,

    Our language arts theme this month is centered around plants. This week we are learning about seeds. Your child needs to bring a picture of something that grows from a seed. You may help your child draw or find a picture in a magazine. Please return the picture tomorrow.

Thank you for helping!

A follow-up activity might include sorting and classifying these pictures according to whether the plant produces food or not, i.e., flower, grapes, oak tree, oranges, etc. A booklet can then be made including all the homework pictures or individual booklets may be made from each classification.

---

1. Baratta-Lorton, Mary. **Mathematics Their Way**, Addison-Wesley Publishing Company, Reading, MA.
2. Available through *Teaching Resource Center*, P.O. Box 1509, San Leandro, CA 94577.

 *Crazy Color Creatures*

 # Materials

- Blacklines 1–10 for the big book.
- Blacklines 11–13 for the pocket chart
- Felt pens
- Sentence strips
- Laminating film or contact paper
- One loose leaf binder ring
- A 12″ x 18″ piece of each of the following colors of construction paper for the big book: red, orange, blue, yellow, black, brown, white, pink, and purple
- Song, *Colors* from the record, *Learning Basic Skills Through Music, Volume I,* by Hap Palmer
- Song, *Parade Of Colors* from the record, *Learning Basic Skills Through Music, Volume II,* by Hap Palmer
- Blackline 14 for the *Rhyme Time Class Book*

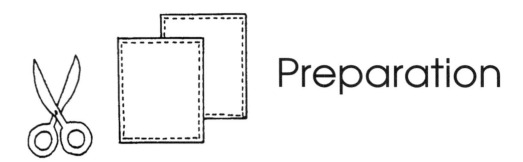

Preparation

1. Color and cut the pocket chart pictures, blacklines 11–13. Laminate or contact.
2. Text for the big book is as follows:

Fred Red bumps his head.

Mel O. Yellow plays the cello.

Jean Green can't be seen.

Sue Blue has the flu.

Merple Purple loves to slurple.

Dwight White stays up all night.

Jack Black sits on a tack.

Round Brown flies to town.

Linc Pink has feet that stink.

Orin Orange can dance the torange.

3. For the pocket chart, print the text on sentence strips.
   Note: For first grade, print the sentences in the corresponding colors and cut apart into individual word cards.

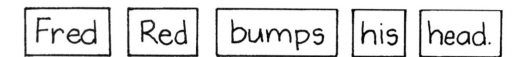

For kindergarten, print each sentence on one long strip or you may wish to print only the color words.

Fred Red bumps his head.

4. For the big book, copy blacklines 1–10. Color, cut and mount the pictures on to a corresponding color of 18″ by 12″ construction paper. Print the text with a corresponding color of felt pen on to sentence strips. Glue the sentence strips on the construction paper. The completed page will look like this:

Contact or laminate. Punch a hole in the lower left corner and bind with a loose leaf ring.

5. Copy blackline 14, one per child, for the *Rhyme Time Class Book.*

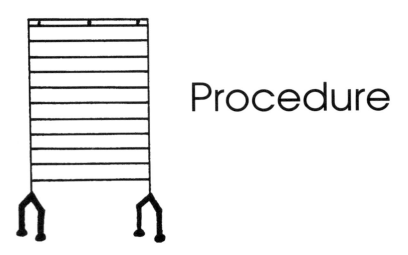

Procedure

1. Introduce Crazy Color Creatures by using the pictures only in the pocket chart. Sing the words to the tune of *Skip to My Lou.*

   Example:
   Fred Red bumps his head,
   Fred Red bumps his head,
   Fred Red bumps his head,
   Crazy color creatures!!

2. Sing again, having the children join in where they are able.
3. Read and enjoy the big book.
4. Read the big book using the *my turn, your turn* technique.
5. Kindergarten–match the color names to the creatures in the pocket chart.
6. First grade–build the entire text. The text could be color coded to make it easier to rebuild.
7. Read the entire text from the pocket chart or the big book.
8. Review the concept of rhyme and find the rhyming words in the text.
9. Orally try to make up other rhyming couplets for the color words.

   Example: went to bed.
   Fred Red   stands on his head.
                    vacationed at Club Med.
                    fell off the sled.
                    loves jam and bread.

10. **Homework:** Ask the children to bring two pictures of things that rhyme. These will be used to make a class book for the extension activity. If you wish to send a note, it might read as follows:

Dear Parents,
    We are beginning a theme on colors and have been working with the concept of rhyme. Could you please help your child draw or look through old magazines for two pictures of things that rhyme.

Example:

Please return the homework tomorrow. Thank you for helping.

Sincerely,

Extensions

Color Song and Rhyme Time Booklet

1. You will need small cards of colored construction paper to correspond to the colors on the Hap Palmer record you have chosen. Be sure to have enough cards for each child to have one color. Follow the directions on the recording and dramatize.

Note: This may be difficult for some children. To make it easier, group the children who picked the same color together:

2. *Rhyme Time Class Book*: Each child needs one copy of the blackline 14. The children then paste the rhyming home picture 6 work pictures and, depending upon ability, fill in the rhyming words or have the teacher write the words for them. Bind the pages into a class book and add a cover of your choice.

Activity 2

Ollie's Outing

Materials

- Blacklines 21–34 for the big book of *Ollie's Outing*
- Blacklines 15–18 for the pocket chart
- Blacklines 19–20 for the class book
- *The Snail's Spell* by Joanne Ryder
- Sentence strips
- Felt pens
- Contact paper or laminating film
- 6″ x 4½″ pieces of colored construction paper to correspond to the text, to be used as color swatches
- Loose leaf rings

Preparation

1. Color the big book, *Ollie's Outing*, blacklines 21–34. Color as follows: gray sky, white fence, green lettuce, brown bunny, red tomato, purple eggplant, black bug, orange pumpkin, pink flowers, yellow butterfly and blue sky. Contact or laminate and bind with loose leaf rings.
2. Color, cut and laminate or contact blacklines 15–18 for the pocket chart pictures. Refer to *Ollie's Outing* for the correct colors.
3. Using sentence strips, prepare a set of color words. Print each color with the corresponding colored felt pen. This will give you two sets of color words—one in black that is found on blacklines 17–18 and the colored set you made.
4. Copy blackline 19, the booklet cover, on tan construction paper. Staple this to a blank piece of tan, cut, and you will have a front and back cover.
5. Copy blackline 20, one per child, for the class book pages.

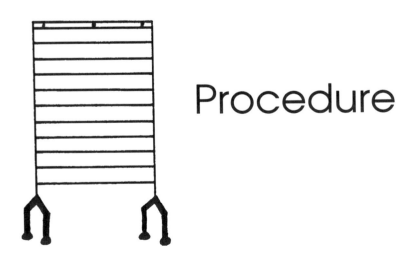

Procedure

1. Ask the children to tell you everything they know about snails.
2. Read and enjoy *The Snail's Spell*, discussing the wonderful illustrations on each page.

3. Talk about the new things the children learned about snails. If you have the luxury of time, you may wish to read some other factual books about snails. (One we like is *Snails* by Althea, published by Longman Group, USA, Inc.)

4. Read *Ollie's Outing*, helping the children anticipate what will happen next by using the picture clues found on each page.

5. Read, using the *my turn, your turn* technique.

6. The children read the entire book.

7. The children sequence the pictures in the pocket chart and chant, using the big book to check for accuracy.

8. Distribute the color swatches and the color words printed in the various colors to the children. The children find their partners and place these cards next to the appropriate pictures in the pocket chart.

9. Distribute the color words from blacklines 17–18 to the children. Have the children match these words to those in the pocket chart.

10. Read together from the pocket chart.

11. Distribute pictures, color swatches, and color words to the children. (You may wish to only use one set of color words, depending on the ability of your class.) The children find their partners and rebuild the entire book in the pocket chart. Read.

12. Brainstorm for a color word bank. To motivate this, brainstorming activity, you might ask the following: "What else might Ollie have seen on his outing?" Print at the top of the chalkboard, "Ollie saw _____." As the children respond, record on the chalkboard, classifying as you proceed.

13. After you have recorded eight to ten items, ask the children to tell you where to record the next idea that is mentioned. Continue in this manner until you have several items of each color. This will help stimulate a child's thinking process as well as classification skills.

14. The brainstorming may be chanted in a variety of ways. Begin with "Ollie saw a red apple. Ollie saw a red cherry." etc. The following patterns are also appropriate:

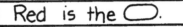
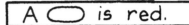

| Red is the ⬭. | I see a red ⬭. |
| A ⬭ is red. | This is a red ⬭. |

Extensions

Class Book and Drama

To make a class book, the children cut out the snail shape, blackline 20. Children choose their favorite idea from the color word bank and illustrate. Depending on the ability, the children complete the frame or the teacher takes dictation. Bind the pages together using blackline 19 as the cover. **Note**: Another way to develop this book is to have the children (as a group or individually) brainstorm for an insect or animal and create their own innovations.

Ollie's Outing   Tillie's Trek   Susie's Swim

Drama: *The Snail's Spell* is a must for dramatization. Reread the book and discuss the things the snail does. Have the children pretend to be a snail and respond through movement to the poetry–like language of this lovely book. You will need very little prompting as the children will become so involved in this activity.

Activity 3

A Color Walk

Materials

- Each child needs eight pieces of 9" x 6" white construction paper for the color walk.
- Blackline 35 for the crayon-shaped book cover labels
- Twelve to fifteen pieces of each of the following colors of 12" x 18" construction paper for making the crayon-shaped books:
  red, orange, yellow, green, blue, purple, brown and black
- A 9" x 12" piece of construction paper in each of the above colors, only this time select the colors in a lighter shade than the large sheets. These will be used to simulate the label on a crayon and will be used for the covers of each of the eight crayon-shaped books.
  Note: Use gray for the black crayon label.
- Laminating film or contact paper

Preparation

Eight crayon shaped books:

1. Copy blackline 35 on each of the eight 9" x 12" sheets of construction paper. These will be used for the cover labels on each of the eight books.

2. Book pages are prepared as follows:

Cut each piece of large construction paper to 18" x 8."

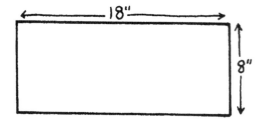

Measure 5" in and lightly draw a line as shown in the illustration.

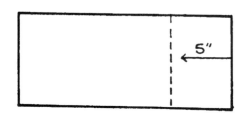

Referring to the illustration, measure 2" in from each edge and mark.

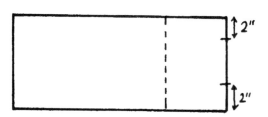

With a ruler draw a line from **a** to **b** and from **c** to **d**. Cut on these lines.

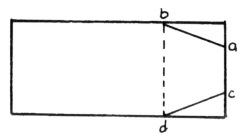

3. Book covers: two each of the crayon-shaped pages will be used for the covers of each book. To make the front covers, paste the labels (blackline 35) 1″ from the larger end of the crayon shapes.

label   booklet cover

The back covers are left blank. We suggest that you laminate the covers so they may be used another year.

4. To make the books, staple twelve to fourteen blank pages between the covers.

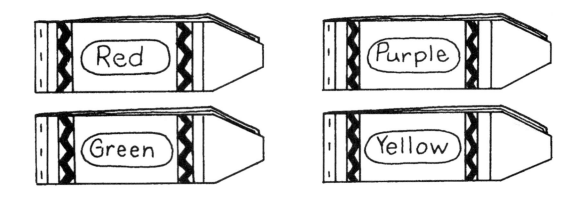

Color Walk:
1. To prepare for a color walk, enlist the help of an intermediate grade class. Each primary child will need an intermediate partner. The older child will illustrate and label for the younger child.
2. Since the older child will be responsible for helping the primary child discover different colors in the environment, it might be helpful to have a short inservice with the intermediate class.

Some things you may wish to discuss are:
- simple ground rules of the walk
- how to give hints to the younger child without actually telling them where to look
- how to give positive reinforcement to the younger child
- how to keep the younger child on task
- the size of the illustrations. They should be as large as the 9" x 6" paper allows.
- how to help the child find something no one else will think of so we don't end up with thirty pictures of green grass!

Procedure

1. Review the ground rules you have established for the color walk.
2. Pair each primary child with an intermediate child.
3. Give each intermediate child eight pieces of 9" x 6" white construction paper and a pencil. (A hardback book or a writing board would be helpful.)
4. Each pair of children will go on a walk through the school and the campus looking for one object in each of the eight colors.
5. As each object is located, the older student draws the picture and labels it. Draw one object per page. Please remind the older child to make the drawing large.

6. When all eight drawings are completed, the children return to the primary classroom. The older child acts as a guide and helps the younger child color the pictures appropriately. When this is completed the older child returns to his/her own classroom.
7. Collect and save these papers for the extension activity.

Extension

Crayon-shaped Class Books

1. Divide your class into eight groups. Distribute to each group a stack of about thirty pictures that were produced during the color walk. Each group sorts according to the color and ends up with a stack of each color.
2. These stacks are then brought to the pocket chart. The whole group chants using the following frames:

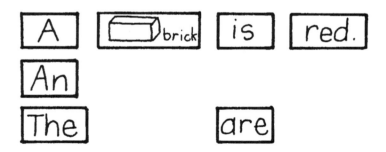

Because you will have collected about thirty pictures for each color, and your sanity must be considered, select only five or six pictures of each color to be chanted.
3. The children now return to the previous eight groups. The teacher assigns a different color to each group and distributes to this group all the pictures of that color.

4. The children cut out these pictures and paste them in the previously assembled crayon-shaped books.

Note: We encourage you to try the color walk as we have described. However, if your teaching situation does not permit, the crayon-shaped books may still be developed. Using the brainstorming from *Activity 2* as a guide, distribute old magazines or catalogs and have the children collect the appropriate pictures and prepare the books in the same manner.

Activity 4

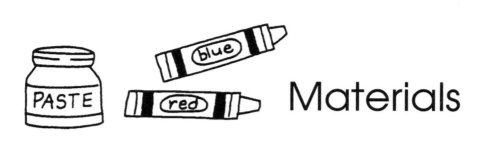

Rain

Materials

- *Rain* by Robert Kalan
- Tape recorder
- Blank tape
- Blacklines 36–40 for the pocket chart pictures
  (There are two blank places for you to color–one blue and one grey.)
- 9″ x 12″ white construction paper for individual booklets
- Sentence strips
- Pan for boiling water
- Hot plate
- Aluminum foil
- Felt pens
- Contact paper or laminating film
- *Listen to the Rain* by Bill Martin Jr. and John Archambault

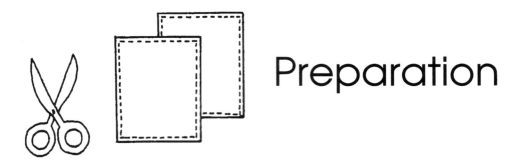

Preparation

1. Color blacklines 36–40 to match the text, *Rain*. Cut and mount. Contact or laminate.

2. Copy the text from *Rain* on sentence strips. Color code your printing to match the text. Example: the sentence about grass would be printed with a green pen.
   Note: For first grade, sentences need to be cut into individual word cards.

3. Print the following text on sentence strips:

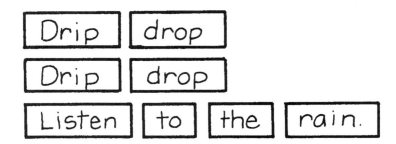

4. Directions for individual booklets are found in the **Extensions** for this activity.

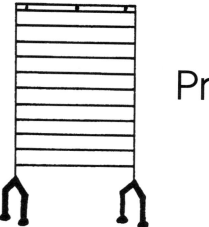

Procedure

1. In order to build on former knowledge, ask the children to tell you everything they know about rain.
2. Make it rain by bringing a pan of water to a boil, using a hot plate. Hold a piece of aluminum foil over the steam. The children will be able to see the water droplets form. Discuss what has happened.
3. Read and enjoy *Rain* by Robert Kalan.
4. Read, using the *my turn, your turn* technique.
5. Place the pictures in the pocket chart, one at a time, as the children chant the story with you.
6. Pass out all the picture cards and, using the book as a guide, rebuild the story in the pocket chart.
7. Pass out all the sentence strips or individual word cards. Working together and using phonetic clues, the children are helped to match the text to the appropriate pictures. Children now read the entire story from the pocket chart.
8. Build the following in the pocket chart:

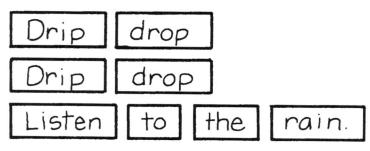

9. Chant several times, adding rhythmic actions such as slapping thighs, clapping hands, patting knees, etc.

10. Brainstorm for other rain words such as splash, puddle, downpour, sprinkle, drizzle, etc. Use these words to rewrite *Drip Drop.*
   A sample might be:

   > Splish, splash,
   > Splish, splash,
   > Listen to the storm.

   Now read *Listen To The Rain* and add words and phrases to the brainstorming.

11. Brainstorm for other things on which it can rain. Insist on a color word with each item.

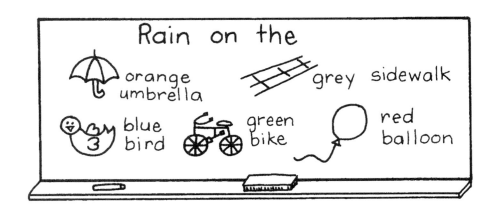

12. Chant all the brainstorming.

13. At a later date, make a strip book of all the brainstormed items. Use your own drawings or let the children illustrate.
   (Refer to pages ii–iv in *The Basic Teaching Strategies.*)

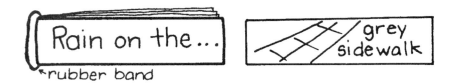

14. Choral Chanting–one half of the class chants the drip drop couplet and one half of the class chants the brainstorming.

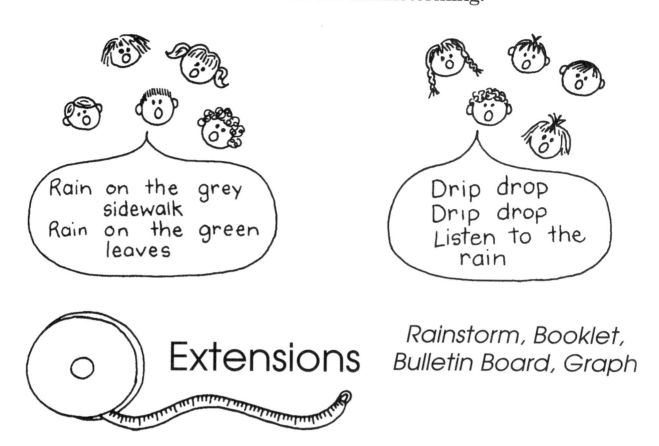

Rain on the grey sidewalk
Rain on the green leaves

Drip drop
Drip drop
Listen to the rain

Extensions

Rainstorm, Booklet, Bulletin Board, Graph

1. **Create a rainstorm:** For this idea we would like to thank a Stockton teacher, Ramona Navarro. Your class sits in chairs in a semi–circle. The children practice the following techniques: Snap fingers or click fingernails to simulate the sound of raindrops. Pat laps, using alternating hands, for the downpour sound. Stamp feet for a thunder sound. Turn on the tape recorder. The teacher begins to snap her fingers, directing the group by passing in front of the semi-circle from one end to the other. The children join in as the teacher passes in front of them. Everyone is snapping. Each time a new action is introduced, the same procedure is followed. The children continue an action until the teacher passes in front of them with a new action.

The sequence is as follows: snapping

patting

stamping

patting

stamping

patting

snapping

When everyone is on the last snapping, gradually have them get softer and softer until the rain stops. Play the tape and listen to the rainstorm you have created.

2. **Individual Rain Booklets:** Prepare the booklets as follows:

   a. To make the blacklines, divide each sheet of ditto paper into three equal sections. (Do not draw lines because this makes it too difficult to cut.)

   b. At the bottom of each section, print one page of the text from the book *Rain*.

Rain on the red

Rain on the green

Rain on the blue

   c. Duplicate, cut apart and collate into individual booklets. Children may illustrate independently, or as a group, using the *draw with me* technique. (Refer to pages x–xi.)

   d. Two possible ideas for covers are:

3. **Bulletin Board**:

a. Prepare the background as follows:

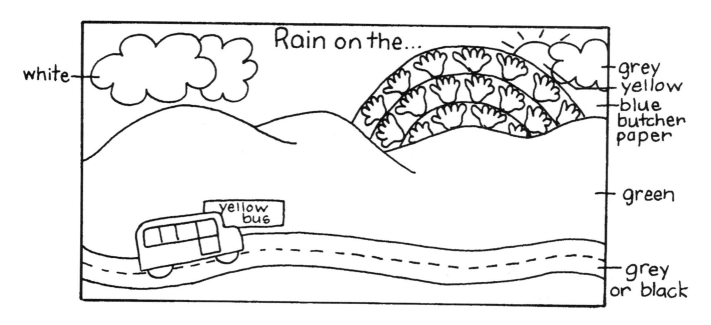

b. Make the rainbow by using the children's handprints.
Either poster paint or colored construction paper may be used.

c. Individual children paint things from the brainstorming.
These pictures are labeled and are cut out and added to the bulletin board.

4. Graph favorite colors.

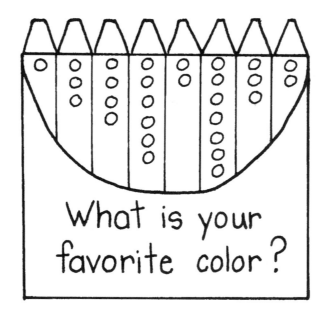

Activity 5 *Rainbows*

Materials

- Blackline 41 for the cover of *I Can Sing A Rainbow* booklet
- Blackline 42 for the last page of this booklet
- Each child needs a 4″ x 4″ piece of each of the following colors of construction paper to make the pages for the above booklet: red, yellow, pink, green, purple, orange and blue
- Drinking straws, one per child
- Prisms, if available
- 12″ x 9″ white construction paper for the cloud, two per child
- Each child needs a 9″ x 1″ strip of the following colors of construction paper for the rainbow mobile: red, orange, yellow, green, blue, purple.
- Small bowl
- Small mirror
- For the big book–two pieces of 9″ x 12″ construction paper in the following colors: red, yellow, pink, blue, green, purple and orange
- You will also need thirteen pieces of white.
- Blacklines 43–53 to go along with the above big book

Note: Illustrated sentence strips and a song tape of *Sing A Rainbow* is available from **Teaching Resource Center,** P.O. Box 1509, San Leandro, CA 94577

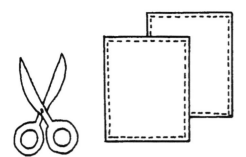

Preparation

1. Duplicate blackline 41 on white construction paper, one per child, for the *I Can Sing A Rainbow* cover. Staple a blank sheet of white construction paper behind so that both covers will be the same size.

2. Copy blackline 42 of the words for the individual booklets on white construction paper. Cut apart.

3. Words to this song are as follows:

> **Red and**
> **Yellow and**
> **Pink and**
> **Green,**
> **Purple and**
> **Orange and**
> **Blue,**
> **I can sing a rainbow,**
> **Sing a rainbow,**
> **Sing a rainbow too.**
> **Listen with your eyes,**
> **Listen with your eyes and**
> **Sing everything you see.**
> **You can sing a rainbow,**
> **Sing a rainbow,**
> **Sing along with me,**

repeat colors and end this way:

> **Now we can sing a rainbow,**
> **Sing a rainbow,**
> **Sing a rainbow, too.**

3. If you choose to make your big book instead of purchasing it, duplicate blacklines 43–53 and put the book together following the text. For each color page, use the appropriate color of construction paper and prepare as follows:

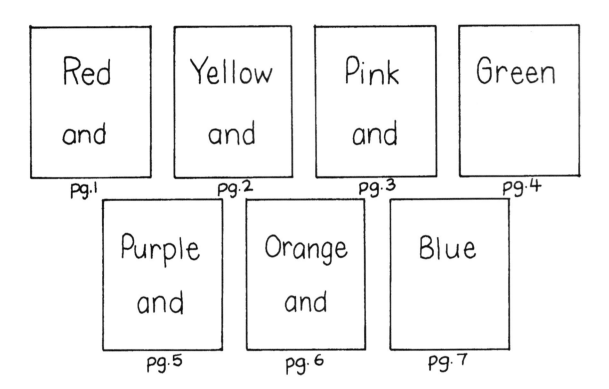

Note: You will need to make duplicate copies of blackline 46 (this will also be used as the final page of the song) and blackline 45 (this will also become next to the last page).

Procedure

1. Teach the song, *I Can Sing A Rainbow* using the big book. Sing using the *my turn, your turn* technique. Sing several times until the children know the tune. (If you are not familiar with this song, look for the sheet music *Sing A Rainbow* by Arthur Hamilton–published by Cherry Lane Music Company.)

2. Read *A Rainbow Of My Own*. Ask: "Where does a rainbow come from? How is a rainbow made? What do you know about rainbows?"

3. Depending upon the maturity of your class, explain how rainbows are made. A book that we enjoy using is *What Is A Rainbow?* by Chris Arvetis and Carole Palmer, published by Rand McNally and Company.

4. There are a variety of ways to create a rainbow. Here are a few of our favorites:

   a. You will need a sunny day for this. Fill a small bowl with water and put a small mirror into the bowl so that the sun shines on it. Hold up a sheet of white paper so the sun that is shining on the mirror reflects on to the paper.
   Be sure to hold the paper still and you will see a rainbow.

b. You will need a sunny day again for this activity, along with a prism. As the sun's rays shine through the prism the light is bent. As the light bends, it splits into many colors and creates a beautiful rainbow.

c. Blowing bubbles offers an excellent opportunity to see rainbows. This can be done indoors or out. We like to put a little liquid dish soap (the kind you wash dishes with) on the children's desks. We mix about 8 tablespoons of dish soap with 1 quart of warm water. We have had success with Joy or Ajax. Glycerine may be added for stronger bubbles but we do not use it. Give each child a drinking straw. We suggest using the small school drinking straws. The children dip one end of the straw into the liquid and blow gently until a bubble is formed. This is a marvelous, painless way to clean the desktops!

5. Sing the song, *I Can Sing A Rainbow* again.

Extensions

Individual Booklet and Rain Mobile

1. **Booklet:** Children color the rainbow and then cut out the previously stapled front and back covers.

Each child needs a 4" x 4" piece of the following colors of construction paper: red, yellow, pink, green, purple, orange, blue and white. The words are printed on the white paper. Staple together as shown. Children enjoy singing the song together, using their very own song books.

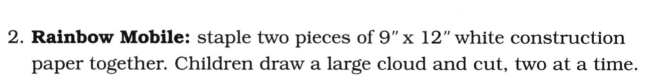

2. **Rainbow Mobile:** staple two pieces of 9" x 12" white construction paper together. Children draw a large cloud and cut, two at a time.

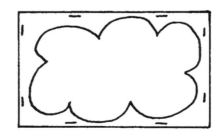

Distribute one 9″ x 1″ strip of each of the following colors to each child: red, orange, yellow, green, blue and purple. The children glue the strips in the order of the rainbow on the bottom of one of the cloud pieces.

Glue the other cloud piece to the one you just worked with, leaving the top of the cloud open. After the glue dries, stuff the cloud with a 9″ x 12″ piece of newsprint or tissue paper. Glue the remaining edges of the cloud together. This makes a great display when all the rainbows are hung from the ceiling.

Activity 6

To Town

Materials

- *To Town* by Joy Cowley, distributed by The Wright Group
- Blacklines 54–61 of things that go
- Blacklines 62–64 for *My Little Red Fiat*
- Blackline 65 for class book
- Sentence strips
- Small index cards for homework
- Felt pens
- Contact paper or laminating film

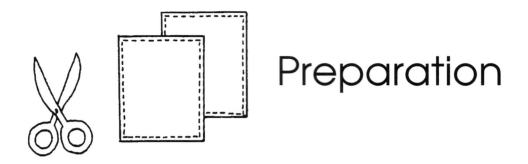

Preparation

1. Cut and contact or laminate blacklines 54–61 of things that go.
   Do not color.
2. Color, cut and contact or laminate blacklines 62–64 of *My Little Red Fiat.*
3. Copy the text of *My Little Red Fiat* onto sentence strips.
   Text is as follows.

> **My little red Fiat needs more gas**
> **How many dollars do you ask?**
> **One, two, three**
> **That's enough for me.**
> **Clean the windshield.**
> **Check the oil.**
> **I'll be home**
> **In a very short while.**

4. On sentence strips, write the following color names: red, yellow, orange, green, blue, purple, brown, black and white. Cut extra strips for additional colors children may choose to add. Depending on the ability of your class you may wish to color code the words or print them in black.
5. Copy the repetitive phrase from the book, *To Town.* Leave blank spaces in place of the color word, the name of the object and the sound the object makes.
6. Copy blackline 65, one per student, for the class book.

32

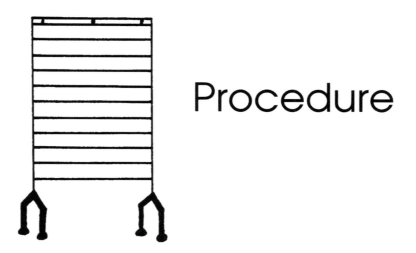

Procedure

1. Teach *My Little Red Fiat* using the pocket chart.
2. Chant and clap, using patchem.
3. Chant, using other colors for the Fiat.

Example: My little green Fiat
                 My little yellow Fiat

Homework: Send home a note requesting the make, color and picture of the family car. A note might read as follows:

> Dear Parents,
>   Please use the attached index card to help
> your child draw a picture of your car or truck,
> and label with the color and vehicle name.
> Please return this picture tomorrow.
>
>   Sincerely,

Note: You will need these pictures for the rest of the activity.

4. Using the pocket chart, substitute the children's pictures in place of the Fiat and add appropriate color words. Chant.

   Example: My little blue Oldsmobile
                    My little brown Volvo

5. Discuss the front and back cover of the book *To Town* predicting what will be in the story.
6. Read and enjoy *To Town*
7. Read again with the children joining in with the vehicle noises.
8. Read, using the *my turn, your turn* technique.
9. The children read the entire book.
10. Brainstorm for other ways to go to town. At the top of the chalkboard print the following:

   I will go to town in/on _____

   As the children respond, record on the chalkboard, classifying as you proceed. After eight to ten items have been recorded, ask the children where to record the next idea that is mentioned. Continue in this manner until many items have been brainstormed and classified.

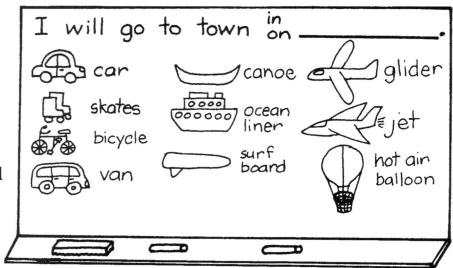

11. Chant. Using the repeated phrase from the book, the children choose different ideas from the brainstorming. They will need to add a color word to maintain the rhythm. Before the extension activities, transfer the brainstorming onto individual tagboard cards. (You may use blacklines 54–61 for additional ideas.) ***Do not color!!***

34

Extensions

1. **Sorting and classifying** (Refer to page iv in the *Basic Teaching Strategies* for details.) Possible ways to sort the pictures of things that go include:

   land, water, air
   number of wheels
   whether you ride **in** it or ride **on** it
   number of occupants

2. **Class book**:
   a. In the pocket chart, place the frame of the repetitive phrase from *To Town.*
   b. Using your cards from the brainstorming, have the children choose a color word and a picture. Place these in the frame and chant. Let the children take turns creating a sound for each vehicle.
   c. Using blackline 65, the children illustrate their favorite way of going to town. The frame may be written by the children or the teacher may take their dictation.
   d. Bind the pages into a class book. A possible cover might include a street sign.

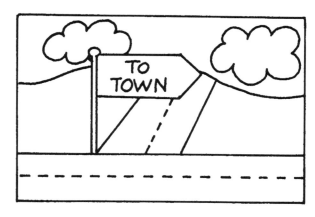

Freight Train

Materials

- *Freight Train* by Donald Crews
- Blacklines 66–68 of train cars for the pocket chart
- 36″ x 8″ piece of white butcher paper, one per child, for the extension activity.
- Each child needs a 4″ x 3″ piece of each of the following colors of construction paper for the extension activity: orange, yellow, green, blue, purple and black.
- Red and white construction paper for the engine and caboose for the extension activity
- Blackline 69 of the caboose and engine
- Contact paper or laminating film
- Sentence strips
- Black sticky dots for the train wheels

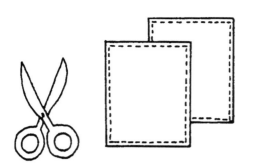

Preparation

1. You may wish to color blacklines 66–68 of the train cars for the pocket chart or duplicate the train cars on the appropriate color of construction paper and then add felt pen features. Contact or laminate.

2. Copy the text from *Freight Train* on sentence strips. You may wish to color code these sentences.

3. Reduce and copy blackline 69 on construction paper for the extension activity. Each child needs one engine, duplicated on white and colored black, and one caboose, duplicated on red construction paper. **Note:** blackline 69 will be used two times.

4. Now color and cut blackline 69 for the pocket chart. Laminate or contact.

5. Extension activity labels–using the book as a guide, prepare a blackline master of the labels. Each label will include the name of the train car and the color. Each label should be no longer than four inches.

black steam engine

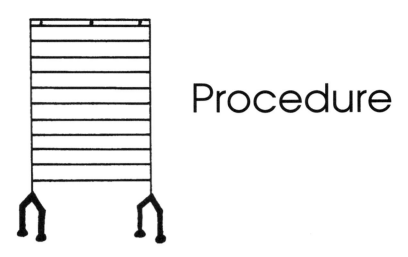

Procedure

1. Sing *Down By The Station* or *Little Red Caboose*.
2. Discuss what the children know about trains.
3. Talk about the difference between freight trains and passenger trains.
4. Read *Freight Train*. Develop the vocabulary as you read.
5. Read using the *my turn, your turn* technique.
6. Sequence the pictures in the pocket chart.
7. The children chant the pictures.
8. Add the text and read together.
9. Ask the children what a freight train might carry. As the children respond, the teacher records by classifying according to which train car would carry that particular item.

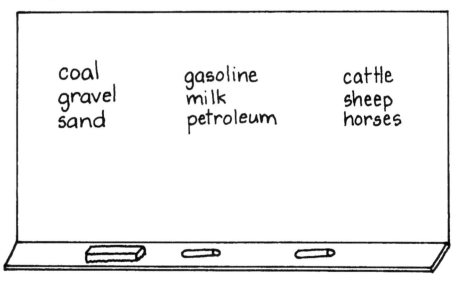

coal	gasoline	cattle
gravel	milk	sheep
sand	petroleum	horses

Be sure not to name the actual car and then the children may guess the names of the train cars when you are finished.
10. Save this brainstorming and at a later date it may be used as a sorting and classifying activity.

Extension

Give each child a 36" x 8" piece of white butcher paper. The children draw a train track and illustrate the appropriate background with crayons, felt pens or paint. The engine and caboose were reduced and duplicated from blackline 69. They may be colored and cut. The remaining cars will be made from the 4" x 3" colored construction paper. The teacher will show the children how to cut the various cars from the appropriate colors. (These are not as hard to cut as you might think. Look at the pictures in the text and it will become obvious!) Children glue the cars down in the order of the text. Add black sticky dots for the wheels. Children cut apart the labels and glue these under the appropriate train car.

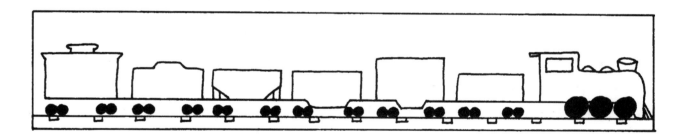

Activity 8

Orange is a Carrot

Materials

- Pictures and word cards for *Orange Is A Carrot* are available from Mc-Cracken Educational Services, 17379 21A Ave., Surrey, B.C., V4B 5E7.
- Blacklines 70–73 of food pictures
- Additional pictures of food are also available from the McCracken Educational Services.
- A collection of food pictures to supplement the food blacklines if you do not use the McCracken pictures
- Blacklines 74–77 for the individual booklets
- 4½″ x 6″ piece of each of the following colors of construction paper for the pocket chart; orange, yellow, purple, brown, green, blue, black and red
- 9″ x 12″ construction paper for booklet pages, nine per child. (See preparation for the actual colors.)
- Assorted colors of construction paper to make the items for the booklet pages
- Cotton balls
- Red sticky dots, five per child
- Googly eyes, two per child
- Small red heart sticker, one per child
- 3″ pieces of dark green yarn for the carrot tops, six per child
- Two or three shades of yellow tissue paper cut into 1″ squares
- Two or three shades of purple construction paper
- Liquid starch
- Felt Pens
- Laminating film or contact paper

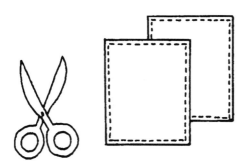

Preparation

1. Color, cut and laminate the pictures and the words cards for *Orange Is A Carrot* for the pocket chart.
2. Color and cut all of the food pictures.
3. Contact or laminate the above cards. Also laminate the 4½" x 6" pieces of colored construction paper.
4. Duplicate blackline 77 of the word strips for the individual booklets. Cut these strips apart ahead of time.

Directions for making the individual booklets

1. **Cover:** Use manila or yellow construction paper for a backing page. Duplicate the page of carrots with the word carrot printed on the actual carrot, blackline 76, using orange construction paper. The child cuts one orange carrot and glues it on the construction paper. Fray three pieces of yarn for the carrot top. Print the word *Orange* with orange felt pen. Use black felt pen for the remainder of the words.

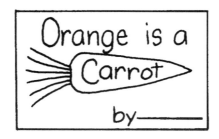

2. **Orange is a carrot.** Duplicate the carrot, blackline 74, one per child. Cut out the carrot and glue it down on yellow construction paper. Add green frayed yarn (three pieces of dark green) for the carrot top. Glue the word strip to the bottom of the page.

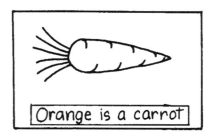

3. **Yellow is a pear.** Duplicate the pear, blackline 74, one per child, on yellow construction paper. Using a paint brush, cover the pear with a thin layer of liquid starch and then add 1″ yellow tissue paper squares, overlapping as you go. Be sure that the entire pear is covered. After this dries, cut the pear out and mount it on purple construction paper. Using paper scraps, cut a stem and a leaf or two. Glue the word strip to the bottom of the page.

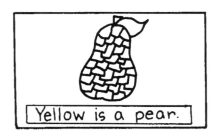

4. **Purple is a plum.** Duplicate the plum, blackline 75, one per child, on light purple construction paper. Give the children two or three shades of purple construction paper to tear into thumbnail size pieces. Glue down these torn pieces on the plum. Cut a stem from scrap paper. Cut the finished plum out and mount on light blue construction paper. Glue the word strip to the bottom of the page.

5. **And brown is a bear.** Duplicate the bear, blackline 75, one per child, on light brown construction paper. Cut out the bear and glue it down on beige construction paper. Glue on googly eyes and add a red sticker heart. Glue the word strip to the bottom of the page.

6. **Green is the grass.** Fringe a 12″ x 4″ piece of green construction paper and glue it at the bottom of a light blue piece of construction paper. Glue the word strip on top of the grass at the bottom of the page.

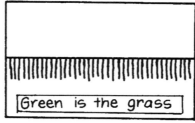

7. **And blue is the sky.** With your fingers, gently spread out two or three cotton balls and glue them down on a dark blue piece of construction paper. Glue the word strip to the bottom of the page.

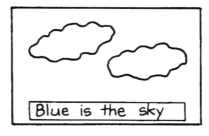

8. **Black is a witch's hat.** Cut a black triangle. Fold the triangle like this:

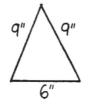 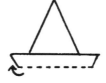 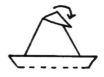

43

Glue it down on yellow construction paper. Glue the word strip to the bottom of the page.

9. **And red is cherry pie.** Duplicate the pie, blackline 76, one per child, on light brown construction paper. Cut the pie shape and add five red sticky dots for the cherries. Glue down the pie on light green construction paper. Glue the word strip to the bottom of the page.

10. **Binding**: Pre-fold a strip of 3″ x 9″ orange construction paper and staple it to the edge of the booklet.

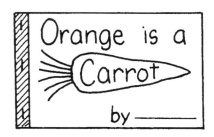

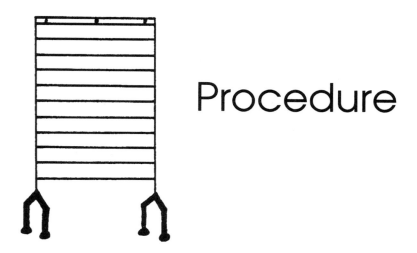

Procedure

1. Introduce the song, *Orange Is A Carrot* in the pocket chart, using the **pictures only.** The song is sung to the tune of *Eensy Weensy Spider.*

2. Add the color swatch to the pocket chart and sing again.

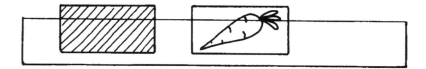

3. At this time distribute the 4½″ x 6″ color swatches and the pictures to your class. The children then find their partners and rebuild the song in the pocket chart, as the class sings.

4. Add the words and sing again. (For very young children it is not necessary to use color words or names of the objects. Simply use a color swatch and the picture of the object.)

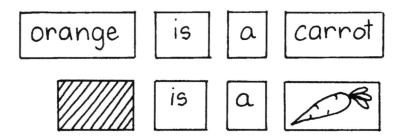

5. Distribute the entire song to your class and rebuild in the pocket chart.

6. Discuss which of the items in the song are edible.

45

7. After establishing the difference between a fruit and a vegetable, categorize the four foods found in the song. (carrot, pear, plum and cherry) Ask the children to brainstorm for other foods that fit into the two categories. You may wish to use the additional food pictures we have previously mentioned.

8. Chant the brainstorming, using one of the following frames:

| A
An ————— is a vegetable. | A
An ————— is a fruit. |

9. Divide your class into small groups and have each group sort a stack of food pictures, according to color.

10. These stacks are then brought to the pocket chart and the whole group chants.

Extensions

*Individual Booklet
and Tasting Party*

1. Make individual booklets of *Orange Is A Carrot.* Directions are under Preparation.

2. Food Tasting—Choose one or two fruits or vegetables from each color and have a tasting party. You may wish to have the children participate in bringing in the food.

Activity 9

Brown Bear, Brown Bear, What Do You See?

Materials

- Book, *Brown Bear, Brown Bear, What Do You See?* by Bill Martin, Jr.
- Blacklines 78–80 for the pocket chart and puppets
- Blackline 81 for the class book page
- Sentence strips
- Thirteen tongue depressors for the puppets
- Assorted colors of 9" x 12" construction paper for the puppets and pocket chart pictures
- Felt pens
- Blackline 82–87 for the bulletin board idea
- Laminating film or contact paper

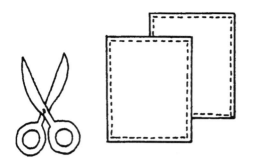

Preparation

1. To make the individual booklets you will need to make your own blacklines. Gradually increase the number of words left out per page until the entire page needs to be filled in. Pages will look like this: (Copyright prohibits us from giving you the actual text!)

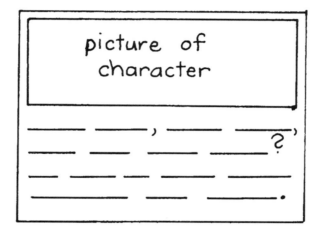

Duplicate one set per child. Collate the pages and staple into individual booklets.

2. Duplicate blackline 81 for the class book page, one per child.

3. **Pocket Chart Pictures:** For each story character, duplicate blacklines 78–80, on the appropriate colored construction paper. Add felt pen features if you wish. Cut, contact or laminate.

4. **Stick Puppets:** Enlarge blacklines 78–80 for the stick puppets. Duplicate these on the appropriate colors of construction paper. and add felt pen features. Cut, laminate and staple to a tongue depressor.

5. Using the book as a guide, prepare the repeated structure on sentence strips.

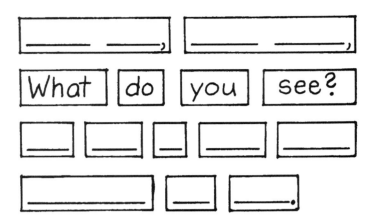

This structure will be used over and over as each page of the text is developed. All of the story characters names will be needed. Each character name needs to be printed three times in the corresponding color.

Procedure

1. Read and enjoy the book *Brown Bear, Brown Bear What Do You See?* by Bill Martin, Jr. The children will join in with the repeated phrases when they are able.
2. Reread, using the *my turn, your turn* technique.
3. **Pocket chart:**
   a. The teacher sequences the story characters in the pocket chart.
   b. The children match the correct names to these characters and then chant.

c. The children build the repeated structure in the pocket chart. As each page of the text is developed, the appropriate words are inserted into the structure and the class reads.

4. **Puppets**

   a. Using the book as a guide, the children sequence the entire story. Use the pictures only. (Leave these pictures in the pocket chart.)

   b. Distribute the stick puppets to the class. Referring to the pocket chart, the children line up in the appropriate order.

   c. The entire story is now chanted with the class saying the first two lines and the individual puppets saying their parts.

5. Have one child stand. The class chants "Susie, Susie, What do you see?" Susie says, "I see Nathan looking at me." Nathan stands also and the class chants, " Nathan, Nathan, What do you see?" and Nathan says, "I see Sandra looking at me." This continues until the entire class is standing.

Extensions

Class Book

1. Distribute blackline 81.
2. On the left side of the paper each child writes his/her first name in the structure and makes a self portrait.
3. On the right side of the paper each child makes a picture of a friend in the class. Each child may fill in the friends name by copying it from a display of class names or simply by having their friend write it.

4. Staple the pages together for a class book. A suggested title might be *What Do You See?*

Individual Brown Bear Booklets

1. Distribute the stapled booklets prepared from the blacklines that you made.
2. Using the pocket chart as a reference, the children fill in all the missing words and illustrate. The amount of teacher guidance required will depend upon the maturity of your class. This is an excellent independent activity for first grade.

3. Another individual booklet that is fun to make is an exact duplicate of *Brown Bear, Brown Bear, What Do You See?* This may be done by duplicating the story characters and the text. You may wish to have your students write their own text. Each picture and matching text are cut and pasted to individual pieces of construction paper. Direct the children to underline all the color words with the appropriate crayon. The children sequence their pictures in the order of the text and these are stapled into a book.

Bulletin board idea
1. Duplicate blacklines 82–87.
2. Using wallpaper scraps or construction paper for the clothing, yarn for the hair and felt pen for the features, the children create self portraits.
3. Write the repeated phrase on sentence strips, inserting the names of the children. Display in sequence on the bulletin board.

| Anne, Anne, Who do you see? | John, John, Who do you see? | Lyn, Lyn, Who do you see? |

| I see John looking at me. | I see Lyn looking at me. | I see Chris looking at me. |

Activity 10

The Birthday Cake

Materials

- *The Birthday Cake* by Joy Cowley (distributed by The Wright Group)
- Blackline 88 for the extension activity
- 4½" x 12" black construction paper, one per child, for the extension activity
- Small birthday candle, one per child
- A 9" x 12" piece of each of the following colors of construction paper: red, yellow, blue, pink, brown and green (for duplicating the pocket chart pictures)
- Vanilla wafer cookies, six per child
- Prepared white icing
- Food coloring
- Chocolate syrup
- Sentence strips
- Felt pens
- Butcher paper for *Yummy Sandwiches* extension
- Laminating film or contact paper

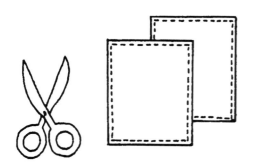

Preparation

1. If you wish to make a big book of *The Birthday Cake*, The Story Box publishers have granted you, as a classroom teacher, permission to make an enlarged version of any story, poem or rhyme that they distribute. (Melser, June, *The Story Box Teachers Book*, Shortland Publications Limited, 1983, distributed by The Wright Group.) Enlarge the pictures from *The Birthday Cake* to the size you wish. Copy the text. Color, cut and mount on tagboard. Laminate or contact.

2. For the pocket chart pictures, trace or duplicate the following cake pattern on these colors of construction paper: red, yellow, blue, pink, brown and green. Cut and contact or laminate.

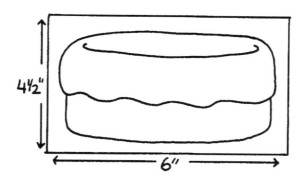

3. Copy the text on sentence strips. Depending on the ability of your class, you may wish to color code.

4. Duplicate blackline 88 on white construction paper, one per child, for the extension activity.

5. Divide the white icing into six equal bowls. Using chocolate syrup to create the color brown and food coloring for the remaining colors, prepare each bowl of icing to match the text.

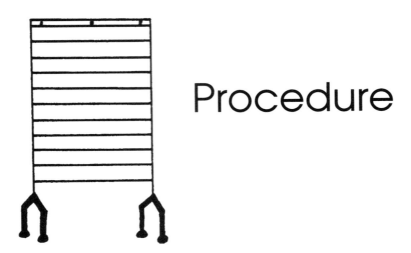

Procedure

1. Read *The Birthday Cake*. Encourage the children to anticipate the number of layers of the cake, the colors, whose birthday it is and where this story takes place.
2. Read the story using the *my turn, your turn* technique.
3. Beginning at the **bottom** of the pocket chart, the teacher sequences the cake pictures and the children chant.

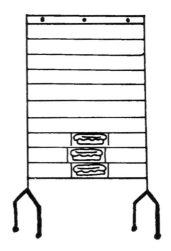

4. The children then match the text to the pictures using phonetic clues.
5. The class reads the entire story from the pocket chart.
6. Distribute all pictures and words to the class. Have the children find their partners and rebuild the story in the pocket chart. Read again.

7. To create an innovation, brainstorm for all the things that could be used to make a sandwich. Sort into colors as you take the brainstorming.

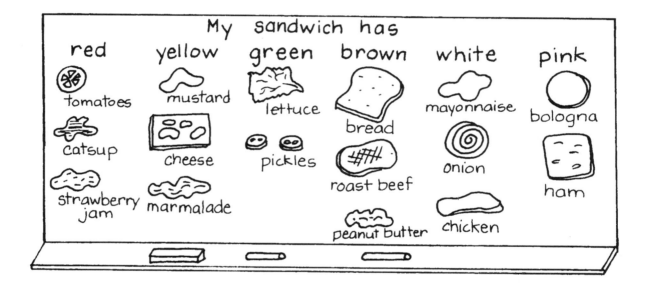

My sandwich has

red	yellow	green	brown	white	pink
tomatoes	mustard	lettuce	bread	mayonnaise	bologna
catsup	cheese	pickles	roast beef	onion	ham
strawberry jam	marmalade		peanut butter	chicken	

Chant, "My sandwich has brown bread, pink ham, green lettuce, yellow mustard..." Orally create several sandwiches in this manner. End each creation with the words, "Yummy! Yummy!"

Note: See the extension for other ideas using this brainstorming.

1. **Birthday Cake Build-Up:** Distribute blackline 88 to the class. The children color each cake with the appropriate crayon and then cut. Mount these cakes in the correct sequence on a 4½″ by 12″ piece of black construction paper. Add the words and either glue or tape a real candle to the top.

2. **Yummy Sandwiches:** Using the brainstormed ingredients, the children write their own book. Depending on the ability of your class, this may be done in groups or individually. If this is a group project, each child within the group illustrates and writes one page. The format we like the best is in the form of an accordion book. Use large butcher paper and prepare as many pages as you have children in the group. The children then glue their illustrations and words to their individual page of the accordion book. Depending on the ability, take dictation or have the children write their own words. The last page should show a picture of the completed sandwich with the words, "Yummy! Yummy!"

3. **Mini–Birthday Cakes:** Each child needs six vanilla wafers and ices each cookie a different color. Refer to the book for the correct sequence. Eat and enjoy!

Activity 11

Red is an Apple

Materials

- Blacklines 89–93 for the pocket chart
- Blacklines 94–96 for the individual booklets
- Blacklines 97–98 for the cover and for the individual pages
- Blackline 99 for the text
- Sentence strips
- 9" x 12" construction paper for the individual booklets
- Contact paper or laminating film
- Felt pens

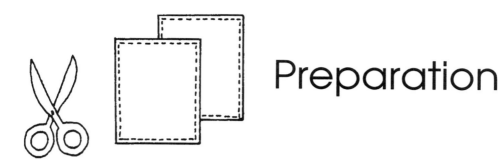

Preparation

Pocket Chart

1. Color and laminate or contact blacklines 89–93.

    Note: there is no picture for "oh so big," "I see outside," and "that is that." You need to make your own for these pages by merely writing the words on sentence strips.

2. Entire text is as follows:

    Red is an apple on a tree
    Yellow is the sun shining on me
    Orange is an umbrella over my head
    Purple is the lamp by my bed
    Green is a leaf on a twig
    Blue is the ocean, oh so big
    Pink is the flower I see outside
    Grey is an elephant I like to ride
    Brown is a rabbit in a hat
    White is white and that is that

3. Print the entire text on sentence strips or, using color coding, copy the text as illustrated:

Individual Booklets:

1. Using blacklines 94–96, duplicate on construction paper, one copy of each item per child.

2. Duplicate blackline 98 on red construction paper for the cover. Staple each cover to a blank piece of red paper. This will make the front and the back cover the same size.

children write
words

children glue on
strip with words

3. Using blackline 97 or 98, duplicate ten apple-shaped pages per child on white ditto paper. If you choose to have the children write the text, use blackline 97. If the children are not writing, duplicate blackline 98. Use blackline 99, one per child, for the sentence strips.

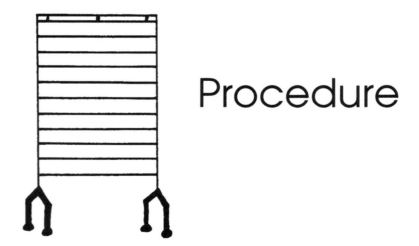

Procedure

1. Using the pocket chart, read and enjoy *Red Is An Apple.*
2. Brainstorm for the rhyming words found in the poem.
3. Read, using the *my turn, your turn* technique.
4. Read or chant the poem.
5. Build the complete poem, one line at a time, using phonetic clues. (Refer to pages vii–viii.)
   The class reads each line from the pocket chart.

6. Distribute all the pictures and words and have the children rebuild the entire poem in the pocket chart. Read again.

   Note: Additional apple activities that are lots of fun to do are listed in the *Mathematics Their Way Newsletter XIII*, published by the Center For Innovation in Education. If this is not available to you, refer to pages 12.2–12.3 in the *Mathematics Their Way Summary Newsletter,* and simply substitute an apple for the pumpkin.

Extension

Individual Booklets

1. **Cover:** Children cut out the red apple shape that was stapled to a blank piece of red paper. This will assure that the front and back covers are the same size! Print the title as shown:

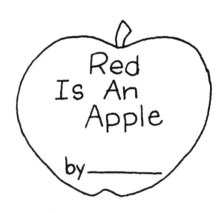

2. **Pages:** For each page, the children need to cut out the apple shape and, depending on ability, either write the words or paste the text at the bottom. Pictures are cut from construction paper, colored and mounted above the writing. Children enjoy using their crayons to create a background for each page. When the pages are completed, staple them together at the **side.** We tried stapling on the stem but the pages **will not** turn!

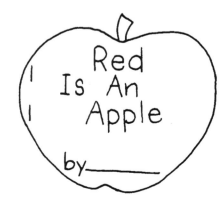

Activity 12

The Little Red House

Materials

- Blacklines 100–101 of the story *The Little Red House*
- Blacklines 102–109 for the big book
- Blackline 110 of the text for the individual booklets
- Blackline 111 for Apple sauce recipe
- Any copy or film of *Johnny Appleseed*
- Sentence strips
- Felt pens
- Laminating film or contact paper
- Floor Graph
- Sticky stars–large gold or red, one per child
- Red construction paper for the chimney
- Brown construction paper for the door
- Circle stencils
- Red Tempra paint
- Apple for printing
- Apple to cut at the end of the story to show the star
- Loose leaf ring
- Sponges for sponge printing
- Green and brown Tempra paint
- Ingredients for apple sauce
- Large white construction paper for the sponge paint activity
- 9" x 12" construction paper or tagboard for the big book

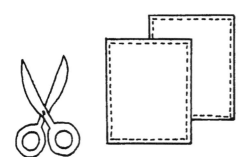

Preparation

Big Book

1. Add color to blacklines 102–109 for the big book of *The Little Red House*.

   Note: We would like to thank Karen Faraci, a Stockton Kindergarten teacher, for graciously sharing her wonderful big book format with us.

2. Mount on construction paper or tagboard and contact or laminate.

3. Use a loose leaf ring to bind the pages in the order of the blacklines.

Individual Booklets

4. Copy blackline 110 of the text for the individual booklets, one page per child.

5. Make several circle stencils from tag (about 3″ in diameter) for the children to trace.

6. Cut yellow construction paper into 2″ squares for the windows, two per child.

7. Cut brown construction paper into 2″ x 3″ rectangles for the door, one per child.

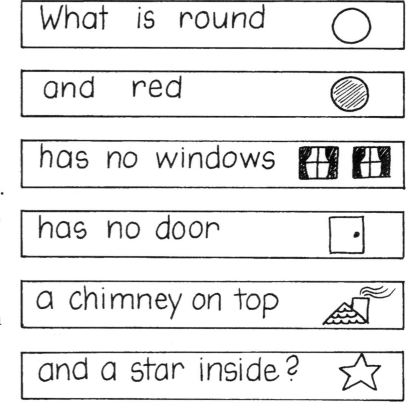

65

8. Cut red construction paper 1½″ x 2″ for the chimney, one per child.
9. The last page needs to be printed with an apple.
10. Write the riddle from the story on sentence strips. Illustrate and color.

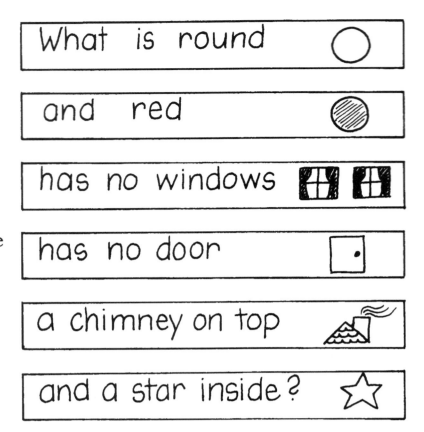

Procedure

1. Using blackline 100–101, read the story *The Little Red House.* Each time the riddle is asked, read and track it from the big book. Encourage the children to join in.

   Note: at this time do not include the last page with this book, as it contains the answer!!!
2. Each time the riddle is asked, brainstorm for possible answers.

3. Complete the story, along with the answer. At this time, have an apple available to cut and show the star.

4. Develop the riddle in the pocket chart, using sentence strips.
5. The children retell the story, reading from the pocket chart whenever they come to the riddle.
6. Dramatize the story with all the children acting out all the parts.

Extensions — *Individual Booklets and Apple Activities*

1. **Individual booklets**–Children prepare the pages in the same sequence as the big book.

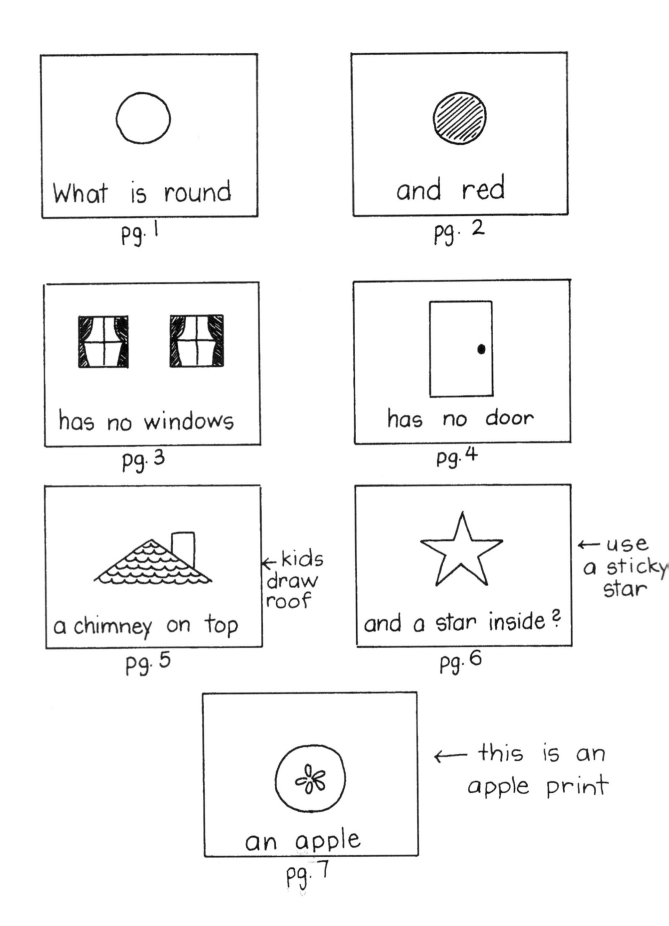

What is round
pg. 1

and red
pg. 2

has no windows
pg. 3

has no door
pg. 4

a chimney on top
pg. 5

← kids
draw
roof

and a star inside?
pg. 6

← use
a sticky
star

an apple
pg. 7

← this is an
apple print

68

2. **Apple Graph:** Refer to the *Mathematics Their Way Newsletter* for apple math activities.

   Note: You may wish to send a note the previous day asking the children to bring an apple to school.

3. **Johnny Appleseed:** Read a story or show a film about Johnny Appleseed. Using a large sheet of construction paper, sponge paint a tree. Dip finger tips in red paint to print the apples. Use crayons to draw Johnny Appleseed and illustrate the background.

4. **Make apple sauce:** The recipe that we like to use is found on blackline 111.

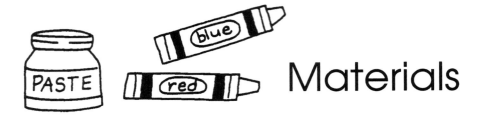

Activity 13

Brown Tent In The Meadow

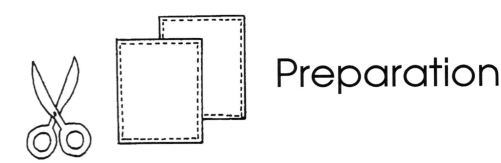

Materials

- Blacklines 112–114 for the pocket chart pictures
- Sentence strips
- Felt pens
- Contact paper or laminating film
- Chart paper (optional)

Preparation

1. Copy the following story on sentence strips:

There is a big brown tent in the meadow.
What's inside?

Black jacket	*	on the ringmaster.
Grey elephant	*	in the ring.
Red nose	*	on the clown.
Yellow lion	*	in front of the tamer.

Orange feathers	*	under the umbrella.
Green blanket	*	on the pony.
Blue leotard	*	above the ring.
White popcorn	*	inside the box.
Purple cart	*	behind the dog.
And pink cheeks	*	on the sleeping child.

2. Color, following the above phrases. Cut and laminate or contact blacklines 112–114 for the pocket chart pictures.

3. Cut each of the sentence strips apart at the asterisk (*).

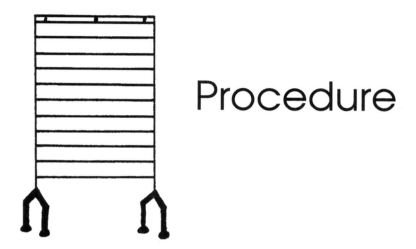

Procedure

1. Ask your children if they have ever been to a circus. Discuss what they saw.

2. Sequentially place the pictures in the pocket chart as you tell the story *Brown Tent In The Meadow*.

3. Using the pictures as clues, help the children retell this story.

4. Display the sentence strips that have the color words where they can be easily seen and obtained by the children.

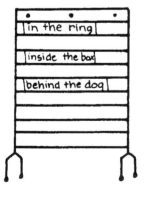

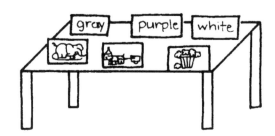

71

5. Help the children match the colors to the appropriate pictures.

6. Read or chant from the pocket chart.

7. Hold up one prepositional phrase (that you printed on sentence strips) at a time and help the children read. Ask a child to put it in the appropriate pocket. Continue in this manner until the entire story is built.

8. Read or chant the story from the pocket chart.

9. Distribute all the pocket chart pictures and words to the class. The children find their partners and rebuild the story in the pocket chart. Read or chant for accuracy.

10. Just for fun! Ask the children to close their eyes. Mix up the pictures and color words. Now the children read:

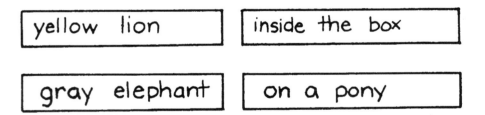

11. Rebuild the story in the correct sequence.

Extension

Rewrite

The setting for this story is the circus. Have the children choose another setting such as the sea, the farm, the school, the wild west, your backyard, etc. Brainstorm in the manner described below.

1. At the top of your chalkboard create three columns with the following headings:

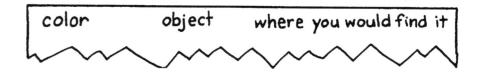

color	object	where you would find it

2. If you choose a sea setting, ask the children to think of things that they would see at the ocean and what colors those things would be. Record their ideas in the following way:

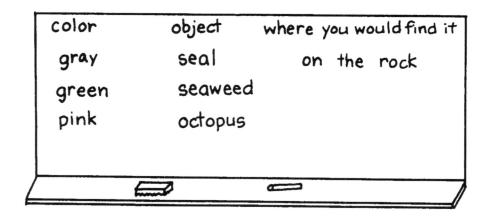

color	object	where you would find it
gray	seal	on the rock
green	seaweed	
pink	octopus	

3. Read or chant all the colors and objects.
4. Now brainstorm for the places you would find all these things and record their ideas in the third column.

5. Read or chant at the objects, including the color and the prepositional phrase for each:

> pink octopus in the cave
> green seaweed in the water
> grey seals on the rocks
> red crabs behind the shells

6. Create an innovation. Using this brainstorming, the class rewrites the book with a sea setting. You might start in the following way:
> Captain Correy set sail and on his trip he saw...
> white caps on the waves
> yellow starfish on the shore
> silver fish near the cove
> pink octopus in the cave
> green seaweed in the water
> etc.

7. Copy the class innovation onto a chart or have the children illustrate all their ideas and create a class book.

The Pirate

Materials

- Big book, *I am a Pirate,* which is available from McCracken Educational Services, 17379 21A Avenue, Surrey, B.C. V4B 5E7
- Pocket chart pictures made from the big book
- Tagboard cards for mounting the above pictures
- Sentence strips
- Felt pens
- Laminating film or contact paper
- Strips of paper to write clues for the treasure hunt
- A treasure
- Loose leaf ring
- *The Pirate* by Pat Hutchins
- Blackline 115 of the cowboy for an innovation.

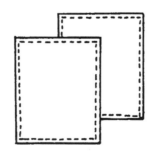

Preparation

1. Permission is granted by the McCrackens to reduce the pictures from *I am a Pirate* to a pocket chart size.
2. Color the big book according to the text. Laminate or contact. Bind with a loose leaf ring.

3. Color and mount the pocket chart pictures on tagboard. Laminate or contact.
4. Copy the text on to sentence strips. (You may wish to color code the color words.) Cut the individual words apart.
5. Treasure hunt—Print one clue per strip of paper. Hide these slips in the appropriate places. You may invent your own clues or use the ones we have listed below:

Treasure Hunt Clues

1. Ahoy me mateys, now listen to me,
   We're hunting for a treasure that you'll soon see.
   Don't fall into the brink
   When you look under the sink.

2. Count to four
   And look behind the door.

3. Look in the bag
   That is under the flag.

4. Find another clue
   In your teacher's shoe!

5. Open drawer number one
   You are almost done.

6. Open the cupboard–no need for a key,
   Is this where you thought the treasure would be?

7. Well, blow me down!
   The treasure is found!!

Note: Clue #2 would be found in the sink, clue #3 behind the door, etc.

6. Hide the treasure. Some possible suggestions for a treasure are foil wrapped chocolate coins, pennies, erasers, eye patches, tooth fairy chests, etc.

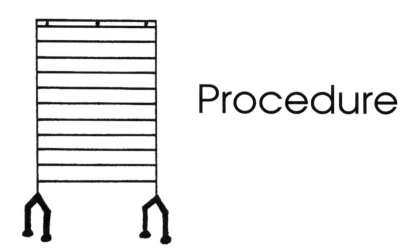

Procedure

1. Ask the children to tell you what they know about how pirates are dressed. You may need to develop some new vocabulary here.
2. Read and enjoy *I Am A Pirate.*
3. Read the book using the *my turn, your turn* technique.
4. Using the book as a guide, sequence the pictures in the pocket chart.
5. Match the color words to the pictures.
6. Chant or read.
7. Working one line at a time, build the entire text in the pocket chart. Refer to the big book for the correct sequence.
8. Read or chant.
9. Distribute all the pictures to the class.
10. Match the pictures to the sentences that remain in the pocket chart.
11. Distribute all the picture cards and word cards to the children. Using the text as a guide, the children rebuild the entire book.
12. Read.
13. As a follow up, read *The Pirate* by Pat Hutchins.

Extension

*A
Treasure Hunt*

1. Go on a treasure hunt. Begin with the first clue and continue until you locate the treasure!

2. Individual eye patches are easy to make out of black tagboard and black yarn or you may purchase them from the Oriental Trading Company, Inc., P.O. Box 3407, Omaha, NE. 68103

3. The book *I Am A Pirate* is fun to rewrite using a different character such as a cowboy, a deep sea diver or a clown. We have included a picture of a cowboy on blackline 115 for you to use for an innovation. (My hat is brown. My lariat is yellow. etc.)

Activity 15

Little Blue and Little Yellow

Materials

- *Little Blue and Little Yellow* by Leo Leonni
- *Mouse Paint* by Ellen Stoll Walsh
- Blue and yellow cellophane paper, enough for each child to have a 3″ diameter circle of each color.
- Tongue depressors, two per child
- Playdough ingredients: flour, salt, cream of tartar, oil, food coloring
- Ziplock baggies, one per child
- Water color or Tempra paints of primary colors
- Blackline 116 of blank equations for recording the color mixtures

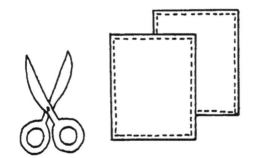

Preparation

1. Copy blackline 116, one per child for recording the color mixtures.
2. Stick Puppets–for each child cut a three-inch diameter circle from yellow and blue cellophane. Staple each circle to a tongue depressor. (Glue does not seem to hold.)

3. Make playdough using your favorite recipe or this one that we like:

> **Playdough Recipe**
> 3 cups flour
> 1½ cup salt
> 3 tsp. cream of tartar
> 4 Tbsp. oil
> food coloring
> (yellow, red and blue)

    a. Mix the ingredients together. Cook on low heat until the mixture *lumps* and then stir into a dough consistency. Store in plastic bags or air-tight containers.

    b. Divide the playdough into three equal parts. Using the food coloring, prepare one mixture of each primary color.

    c. Pinch off small amounts of each of the colors and roll them into separate balls. Each child will need a small ziplock bag in which there is one small ball of red, one small ball of blue and one small ball of yellow.

Procedure

1. Read and enjoy the book, *Little Blue and Little Yellow*. Discuss the story and predict what will happen as the story unfolds.
2. Have the children retell the story, using the pictures in the book as a guide.
3. To dramatize the story, each child will need a yellow stick puppet and a blue stick puppet. Using the puppets, the children retell the story in their own words.
4. Dramatization may also be done by having the children work with a partner, each child taking the part of one of the colors.
   Note: An overhead projector makes this story come alive!!

Extension

1. Review the story of *Little Blue and Little Yellow*. Ask the children if the same thing might happen if other colors were mixed together. Predict the outcomes.

2. Using the paints and blackline 116, lead the children through an investigation of color. Suggested colors to mix:

   red and yellow
   red and blue
   blue and yellow
   red and white

3. Distribute the prepared baggies of playdough. Invite the children to retell the story or create a new one using other colors. The children use parts of their playdough balls to mix the colors.

4. Read and enjoy *Mouse Paint* by Ellen Stoll Walsh.

Suggested Bibliography

Although we have made every effort to locate the current copyright holders of the materials used in this theme book, some we were unable to trace. We will be happy to correct any errors or omissions.

Aliki, *The Story of Johnny Appleseed*, Prentice Hall, Inc., NJ, 1963.

Burningham, John, *Colors*, Crown Publishers, Inc., NY, 1985.

Center For Innovation In Education, *Mathematics Their Way Summary Newsletters*, Saratoga, CA, 1989.

Cowley, Joy, *The Birthday Cake*, Sunshine Books, distributed by The Wright Group, Seattle, WA, 1986.

Cowley, Joy, *To Town*, The Storybox, distributed by The Wright Group, Seattle, WA, 1984.

Crews, Donald, *Freight Train*, Greenwillow Books, NY, 1978.

Ehlert, Lois, *Planting a Rainbow*, Harcourt Brace Jovanovich, Publishers, NY, 1988.

Freeman, Don, *A Rainbow Of My Own*, Penguin Books, NY, 1978.

Gerstein, Mordicai, *Follow Me!*, William Morrow and Company, NY, 1983.

Hutchins, Pat, *One-Eyed Jake*, Greenwillow Books, NY, 1979.

Kalan, Robert, *Rain*, Greenwillow Books, NY, 1978.

Kim, Joy, *Rainbows and Frogs*, Troll Associates, NJ, 1981.

Lamorisse, Albert, *The Red Balloon*, Doubleday & Co., Inc., 1956.

Lionni, Leo, *Little Blue and Little Yellow*, Ivan Obolensky Inc., NY, 1959.

Martin, Bill Jr. and Archambault, John, *Listen to the Rain*, Henry Holt and Co., NY, 1988.

Martin, Bill Jr., *Brown Bear, Brown Bear*, Holt, Rinehart and Winston, NY, 1983.

McCracken, Marlene and Robert, *The Little Boy And The Balloon Man*, A Tiger Cub Reader, Peguis Publishers Limited, Manitoba, Canada, 1986.

McCracken, Marlene and Robert, *I Am A Pirate*, McCracken Educational Services, Surrey, British Columbia, Canada, 1986.

O'Neill, Mary, *Hailstones and Halibut Bones*, Doubleday & Company, Inc., NY, 1989.

Peek, Merle, *Mary Wore Her Red Dress*, Clarion-Ticknor and Fields, NY, 1983.

Potter, Beatrix, *Peter Rabbit's Colors*, Frederick Warne, NY, 1988.

Radlauer, Ruth and Ed, *Colors*, Bowmar Publishing Co., CA, 1968.

Ryder, Joanne, *The Snail's Spell*, Puffin Books, Viking-Penguin Inc., New York, NY, 1982.

Wilkes, Angela, *The Colors Book*, Hays Books, Tulsa, Oklahoma, 1979.

Wylie, Joanne and David, *A Fishy Color Story*, Children's Press, Canada, 1983.

Blacklines

2

13

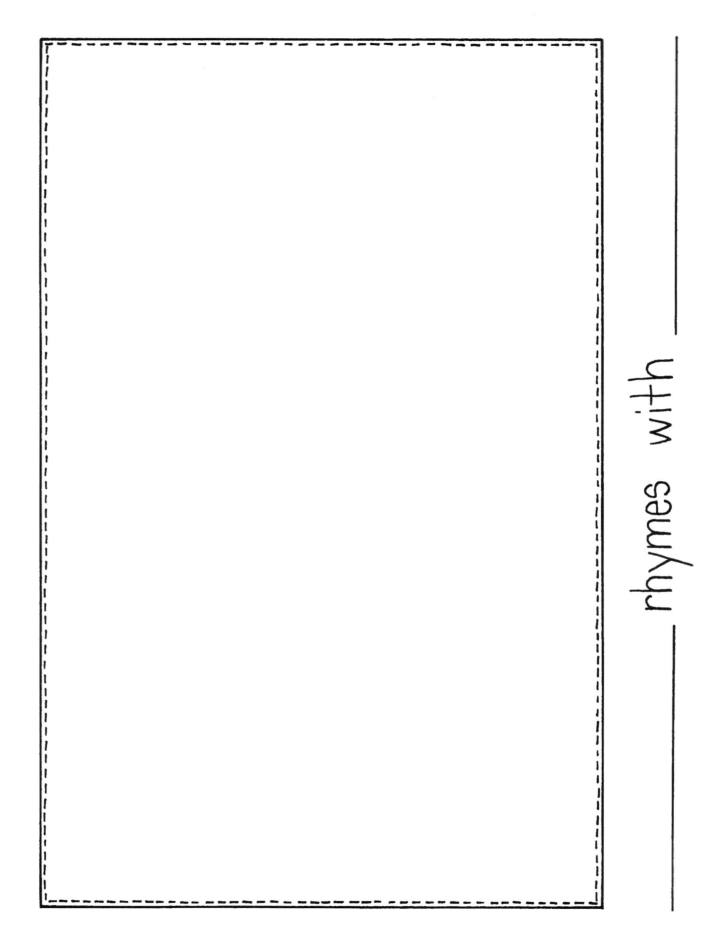

_____ rhymes with _____

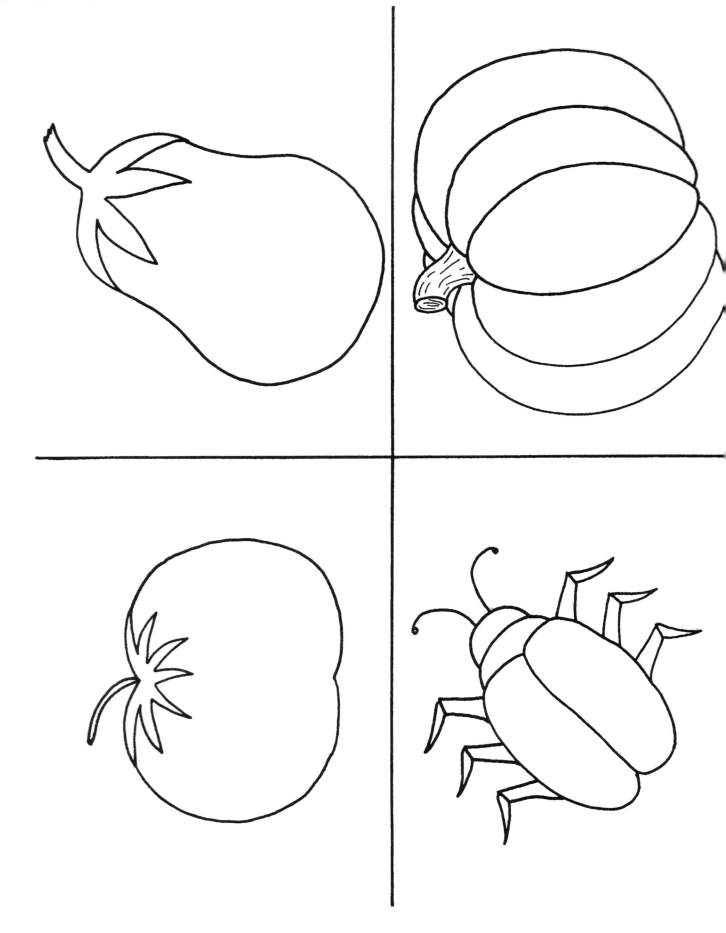

gray

white

green

17

black

orange

pink

brown

red

purple

yellow

blue

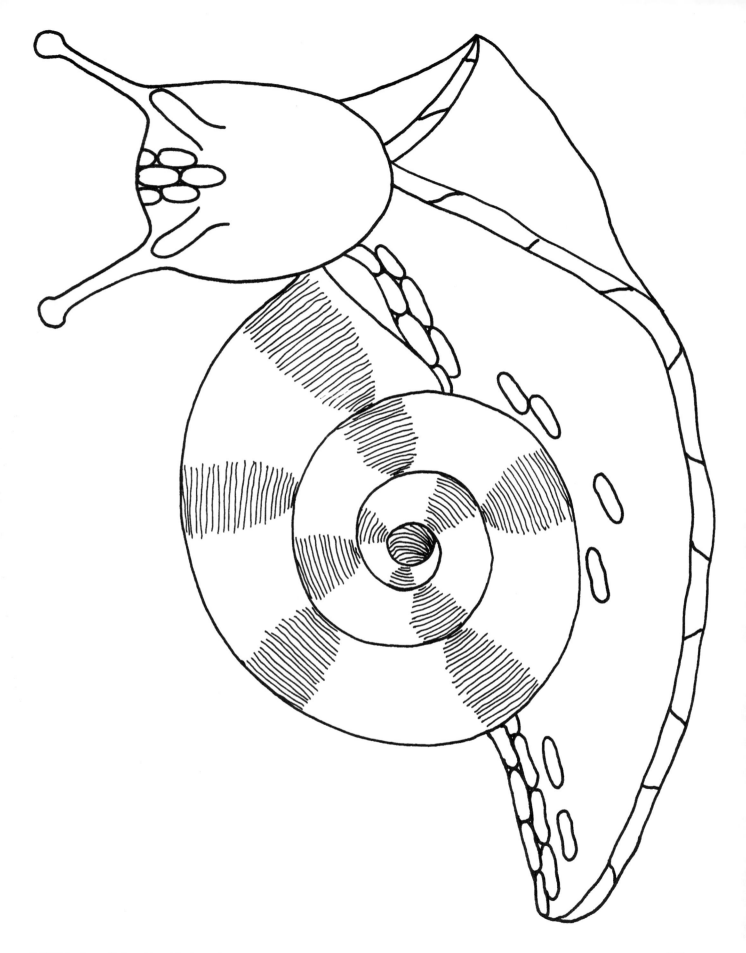

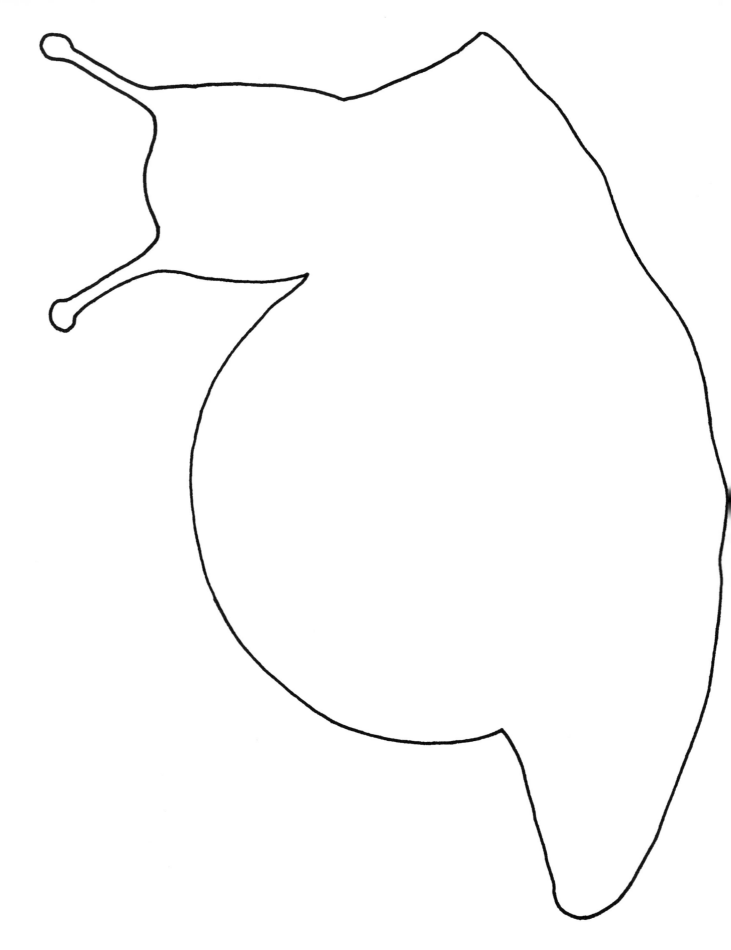

20

OLLIE'S OUTING

By Anne Cotton & Fran Martin
Illustrated by Lyn Hope

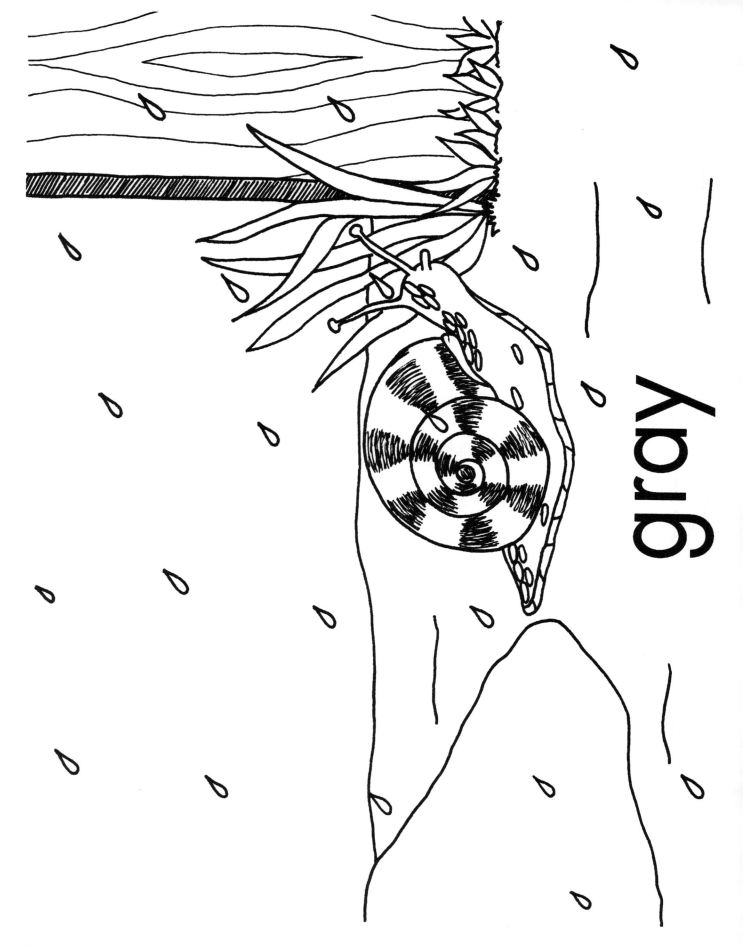

gray

white

green

brown

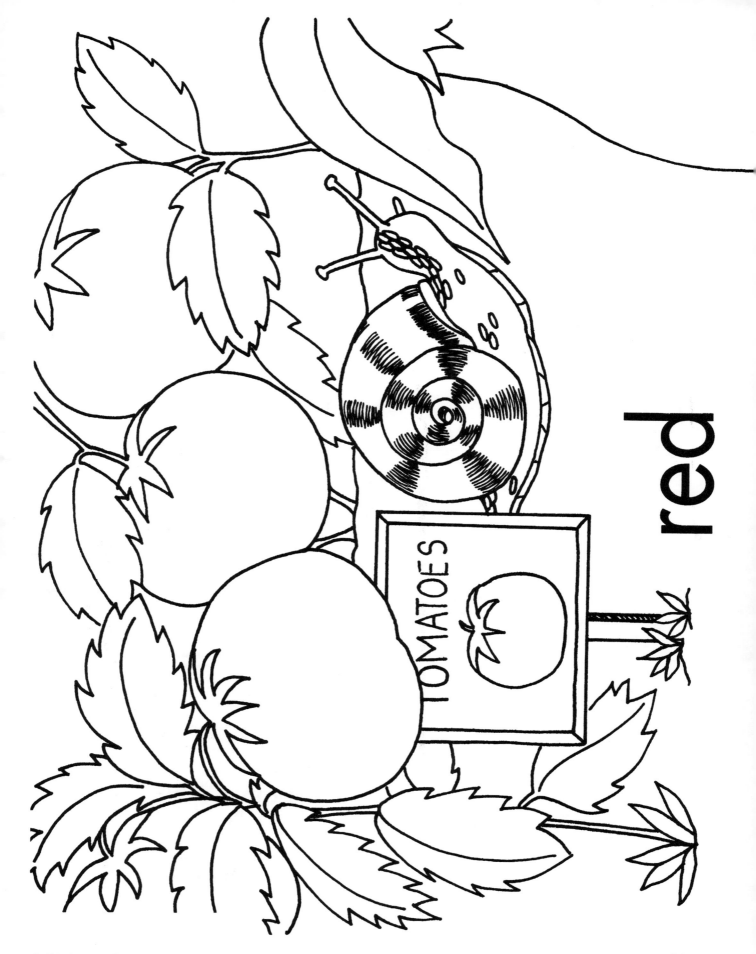

red

purple

EGGPLANT

black

orange

Zinnias

pink

yellow

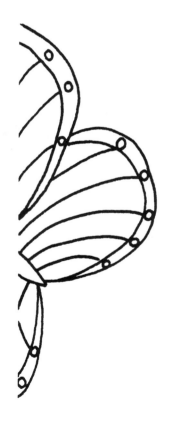

blue

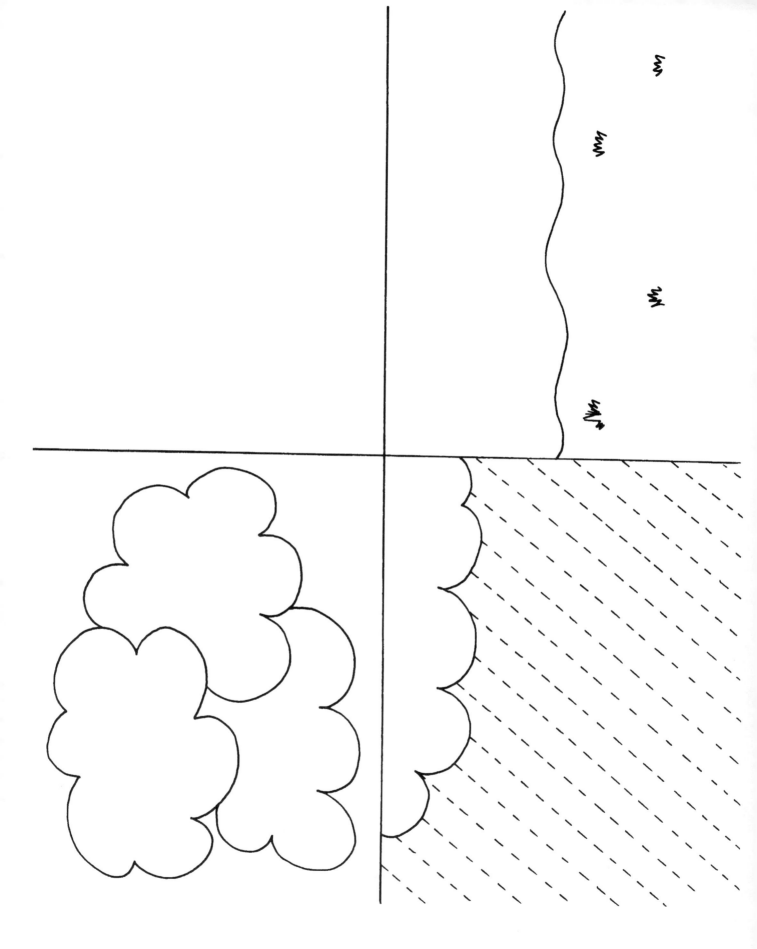

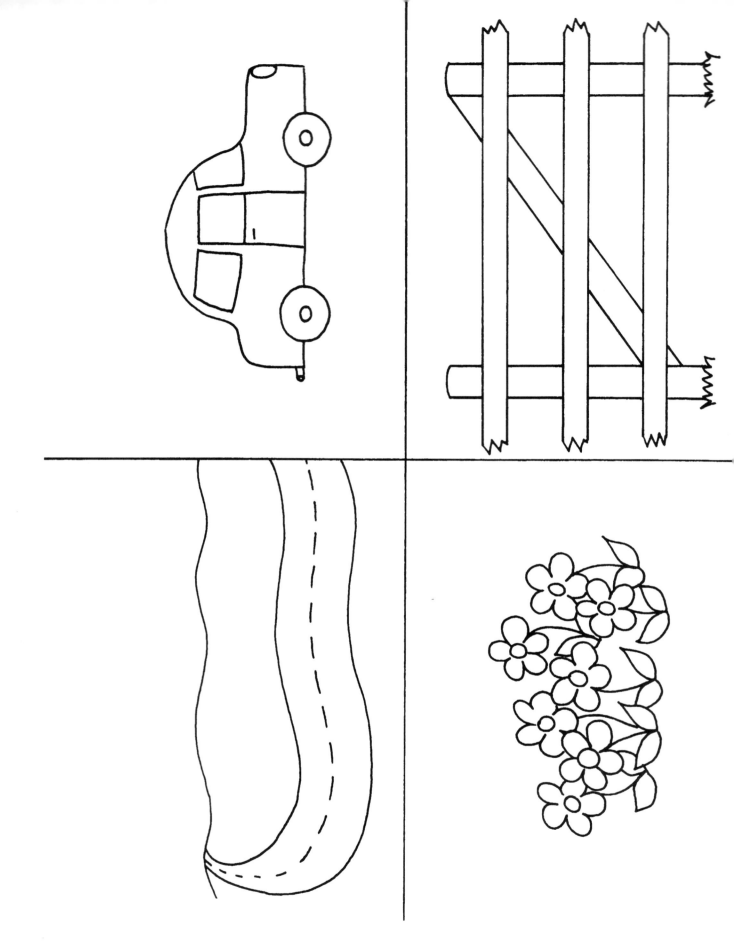

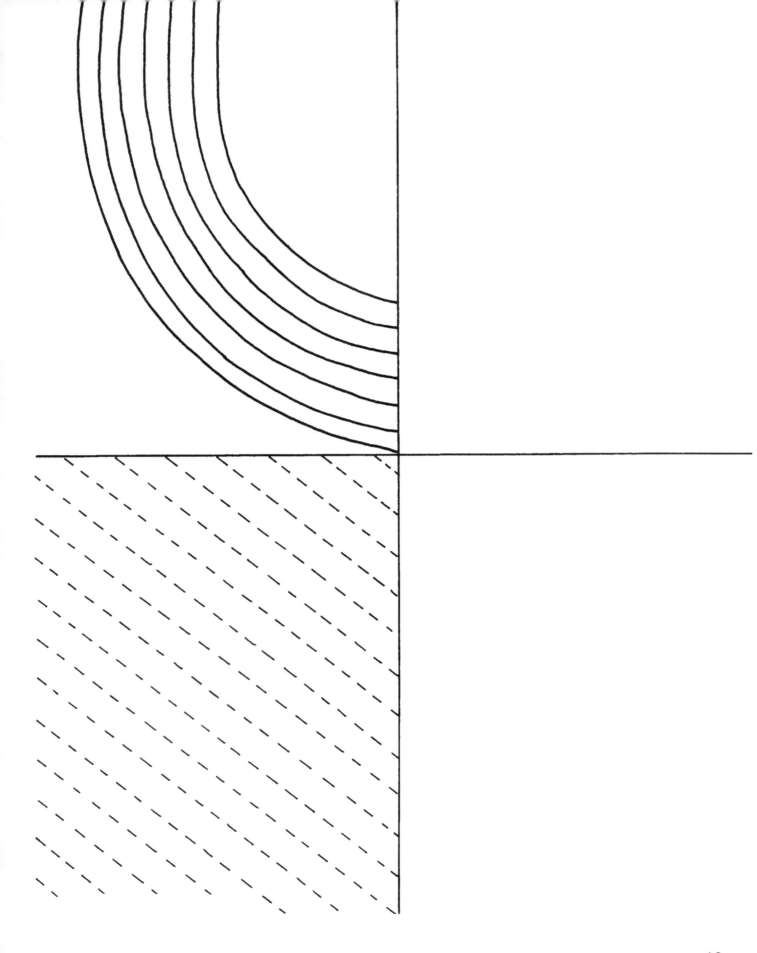

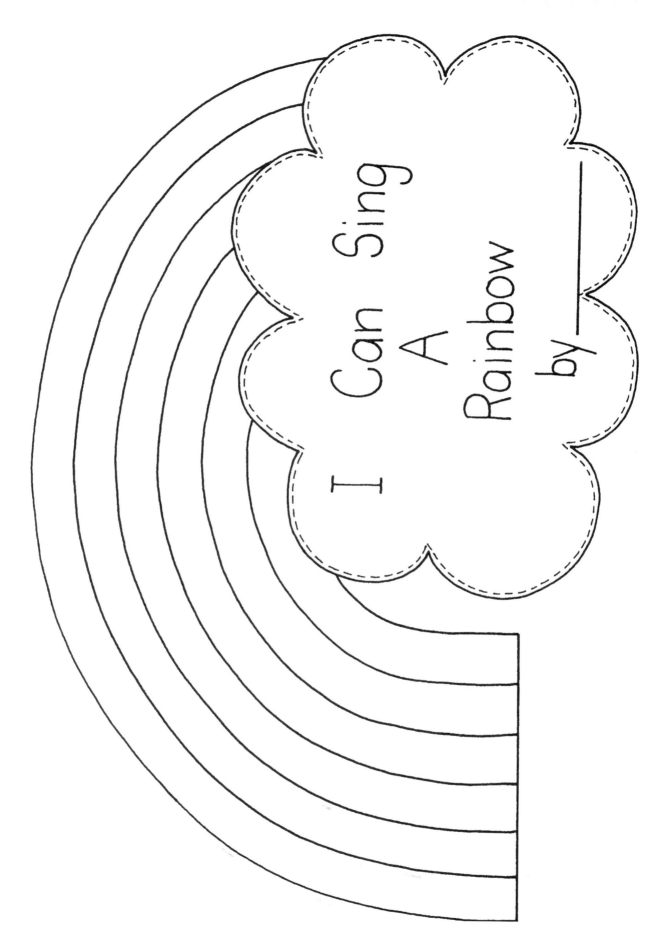

I Can Sing
A
Rainbow
by ___

I can sing a rainbow,

Sing a rainbow,

Sing a rainbow, too!

I can sing a rainbow,

Sing a rainbow,

Sing a rainbow, too!

I can sing a rainbow,

Sing a rainbow,

Sing a rainbow, too!

I can sing a rainbow,

Sing a rainbow,

Sing a rainbow, too!

I

can sing

a

sing

a

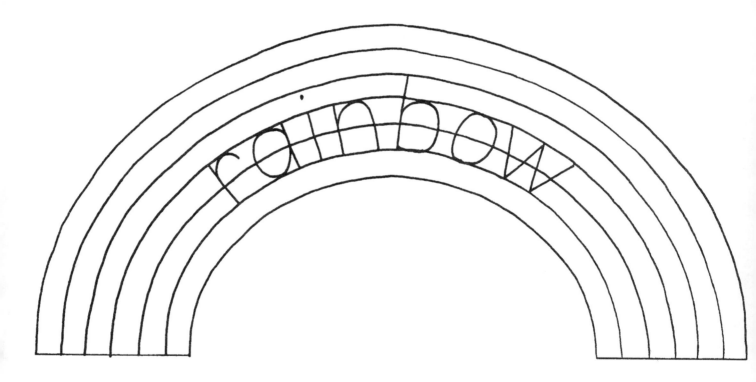

sing

a

rainbow

too

Listen with your eyes

Listen with your

👁 👁

eyes and

sing

everything

you

see

You can sing a rainbow

Now we can sing a

rainbow

sing

a

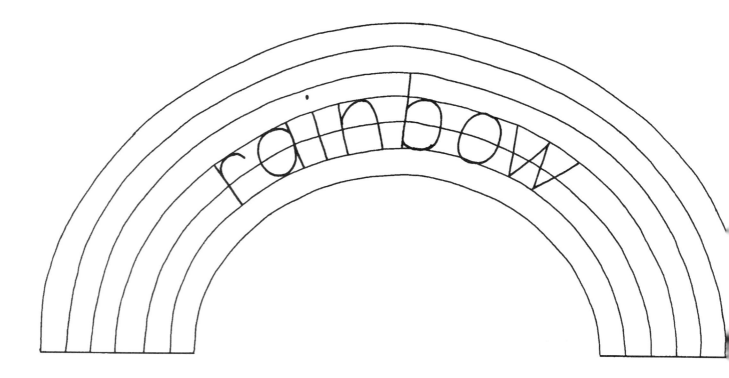

rainbow

sing

along

with

me

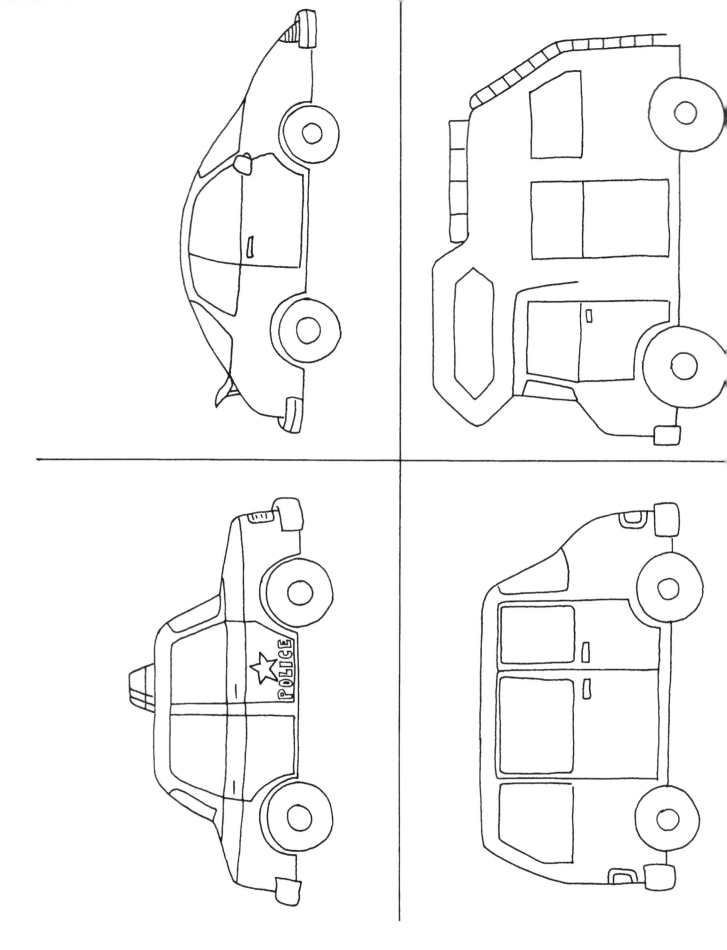

54

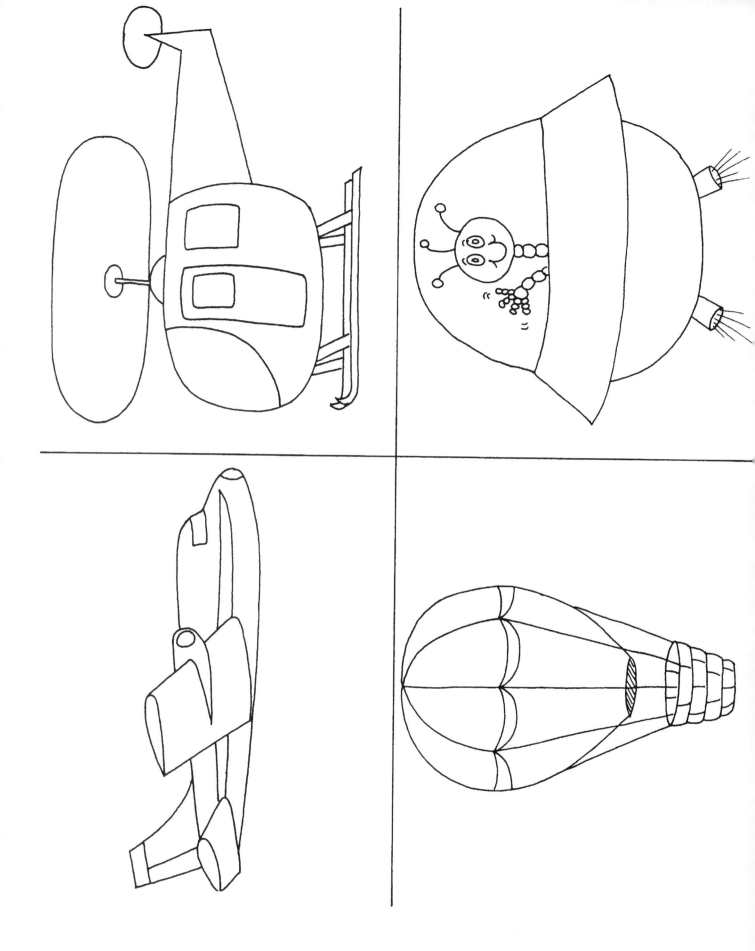

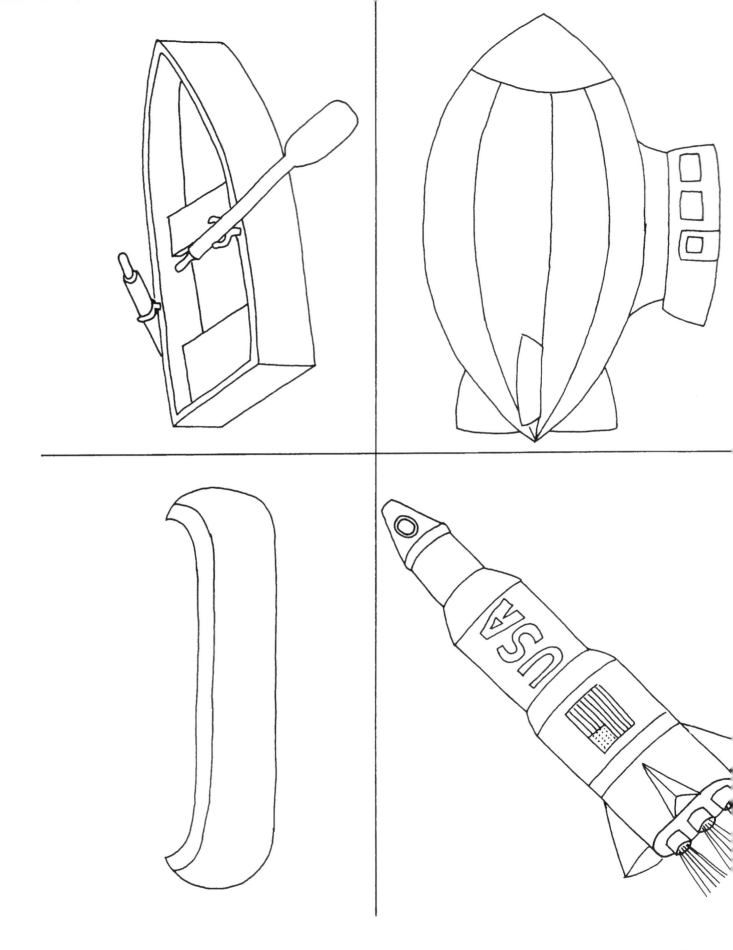

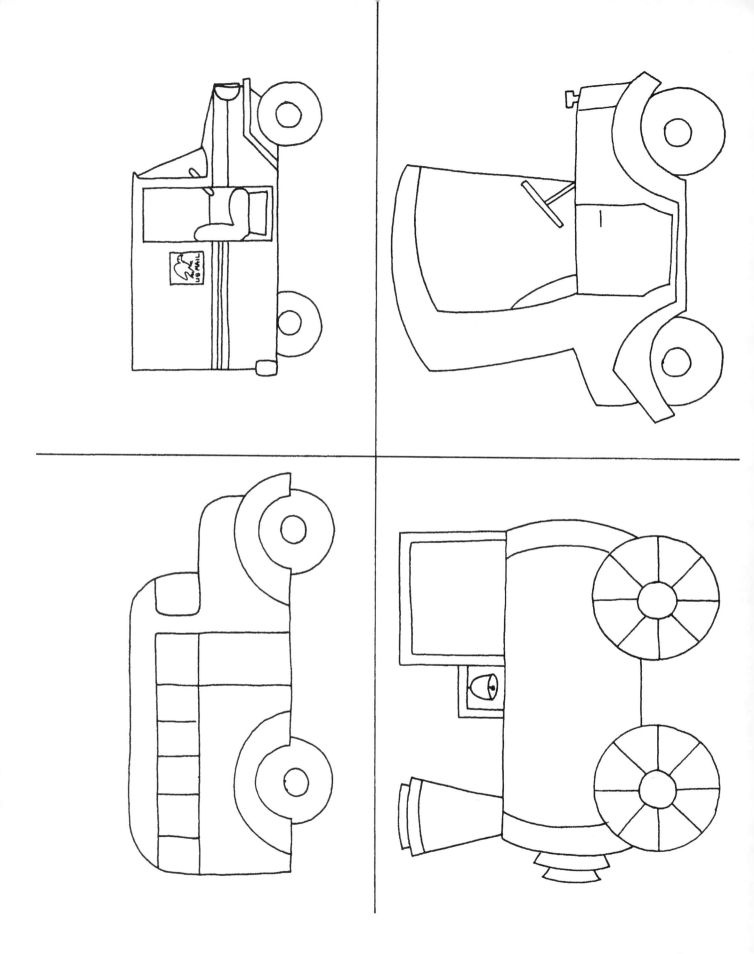

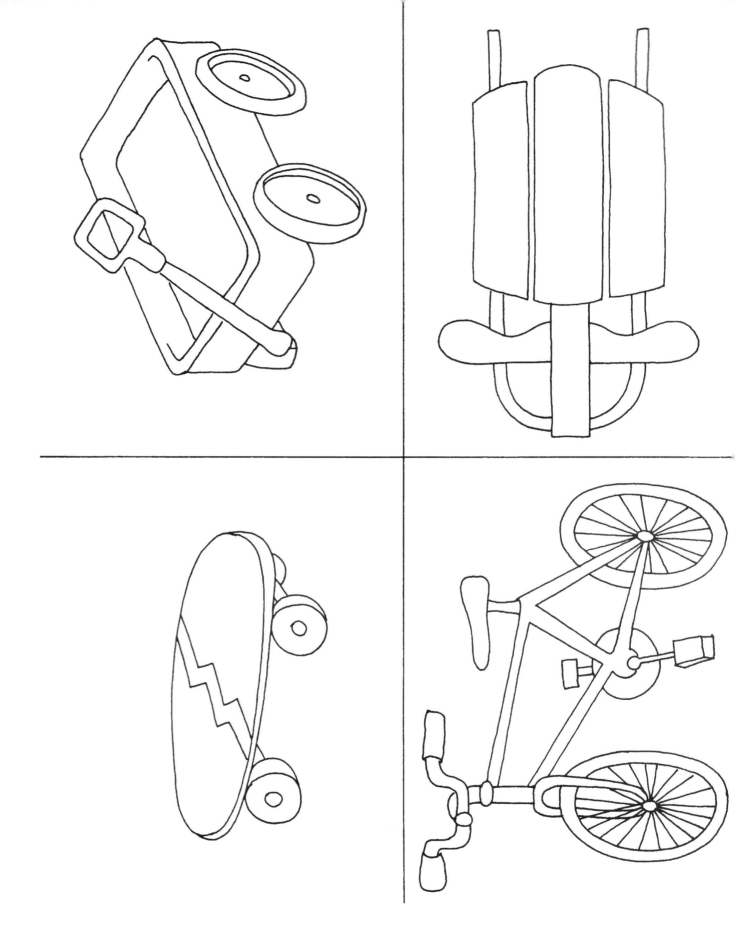

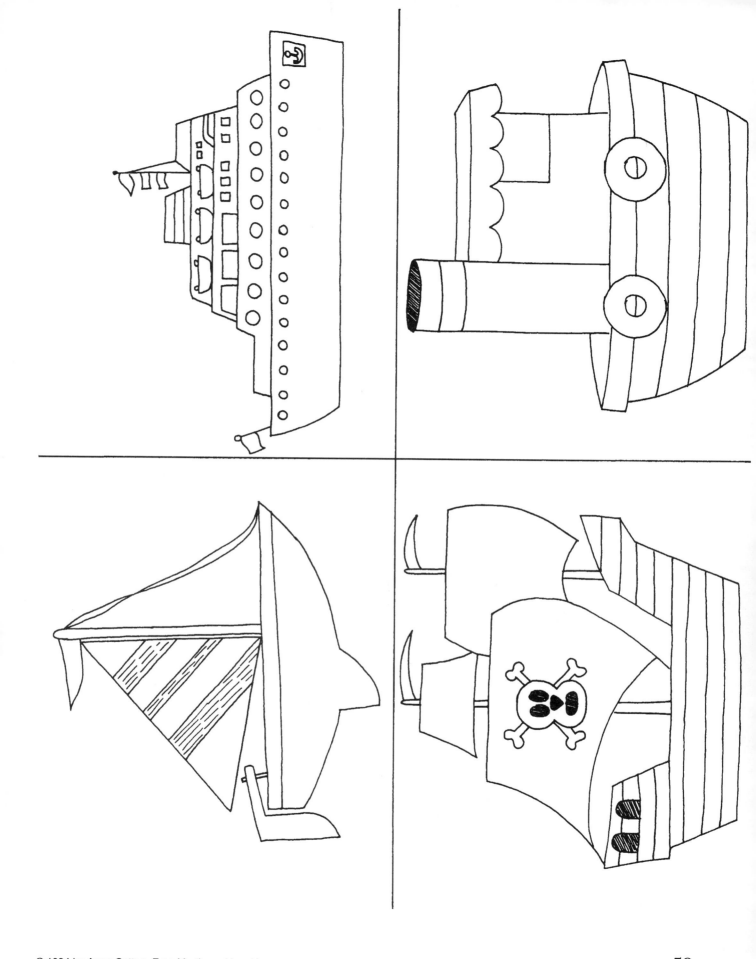

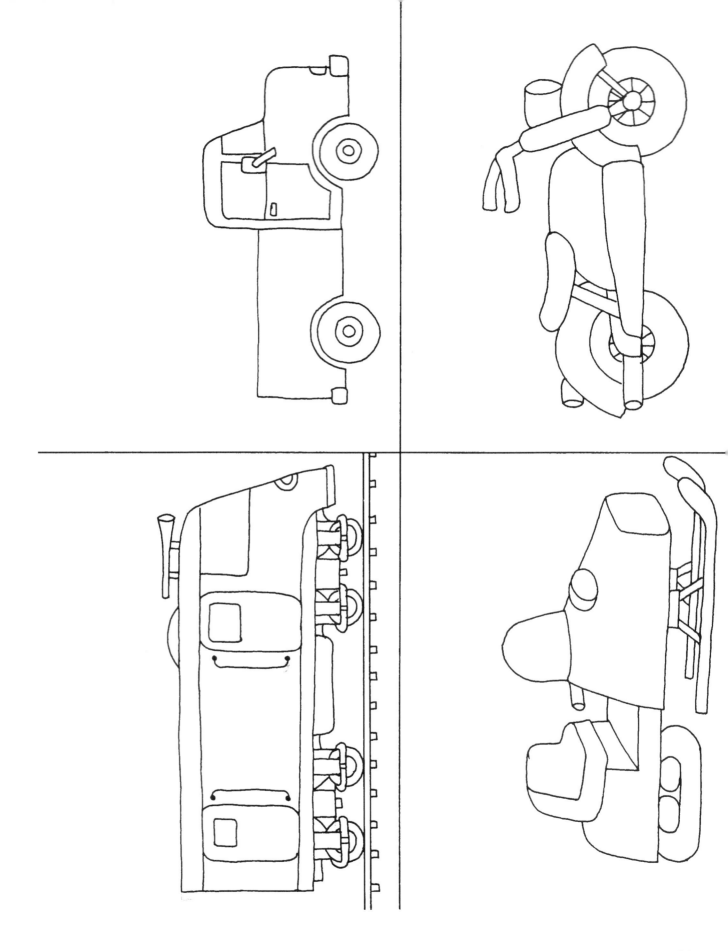

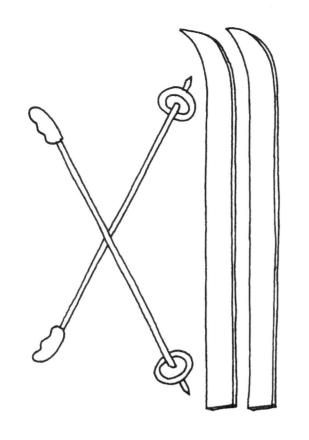

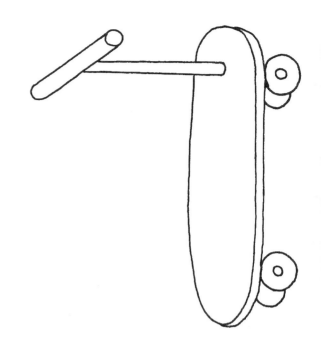

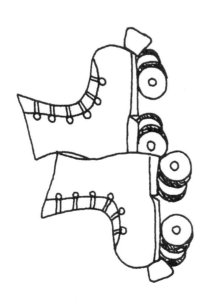

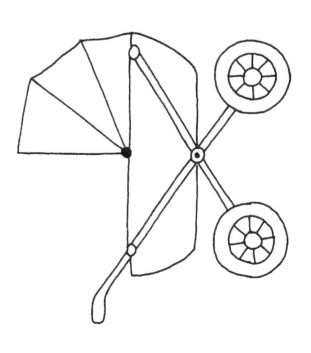

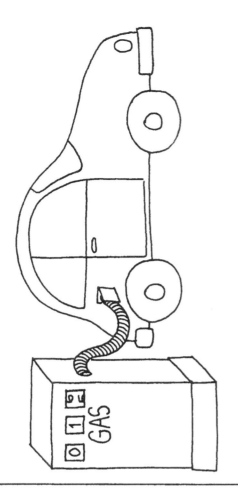

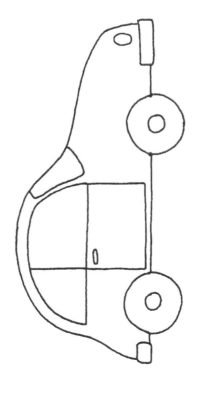

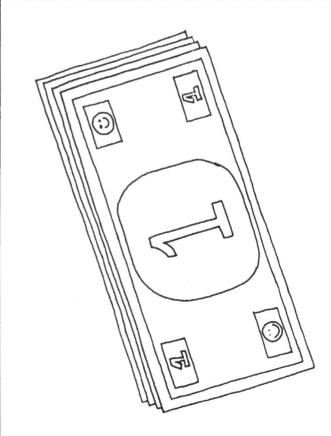

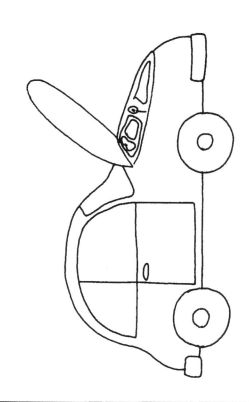

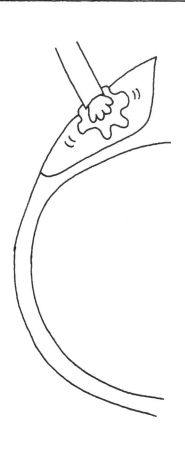

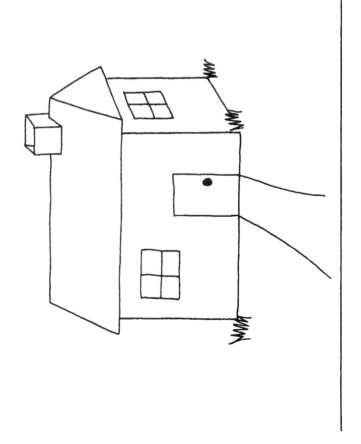

I will go to town

_____ my big _____.

My big _____ _____.

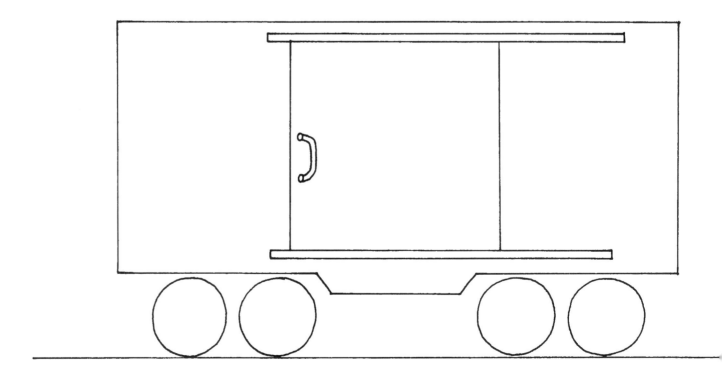

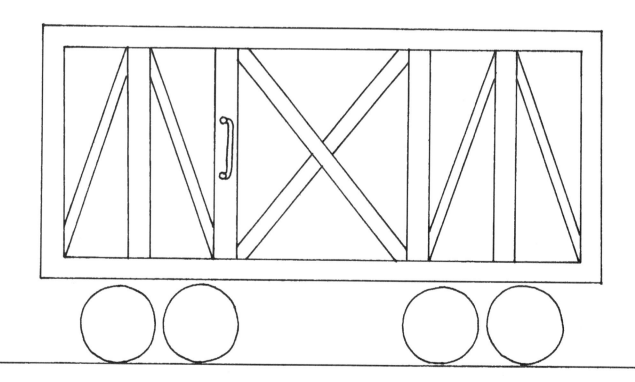

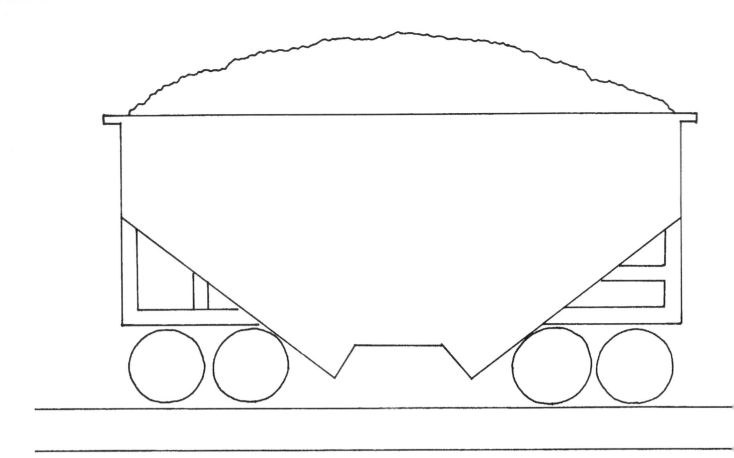

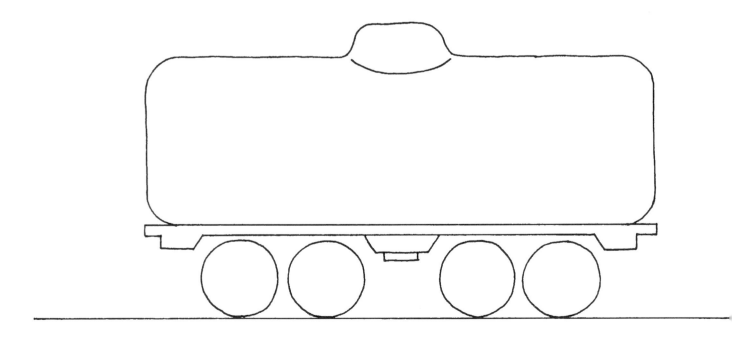

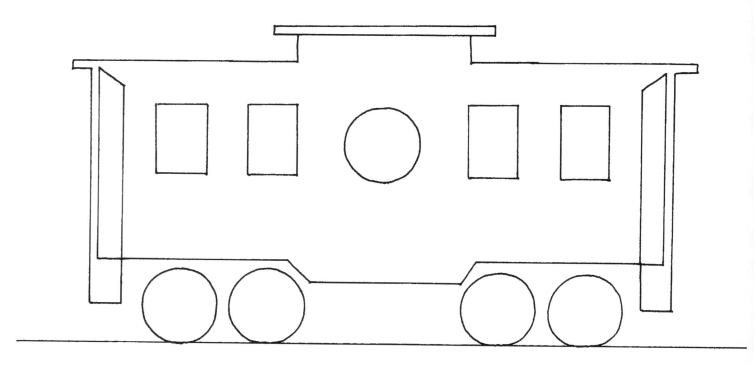

cantaloupe

pumpkin

tangerines

eggplant

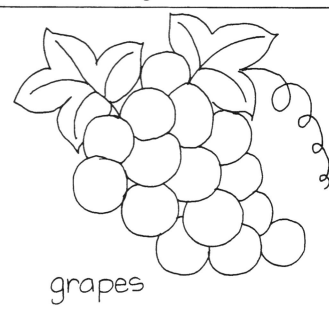

grapes

potatoes

apple

tomato

radishes

strawberries

pineapple

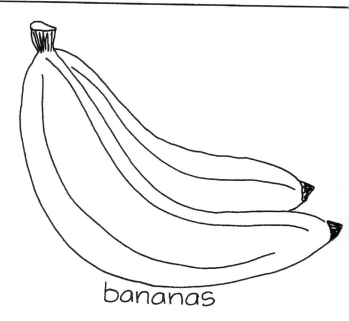

bananas

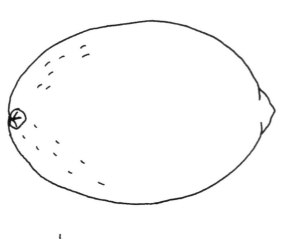

lemon

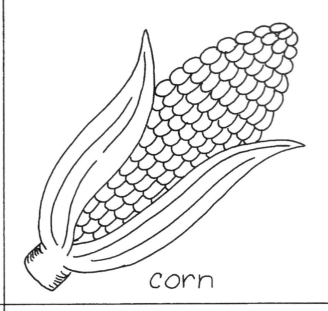

corn

onion

coconut

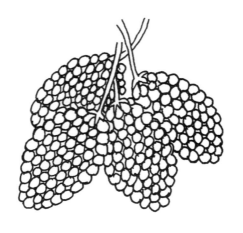

blackberries

blueberries

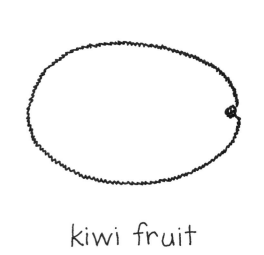

kiwi fruit

beans

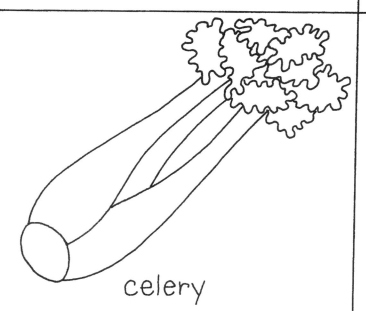

celery

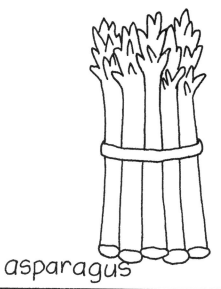

asparagus

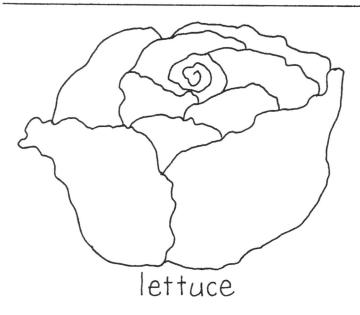

lettuce

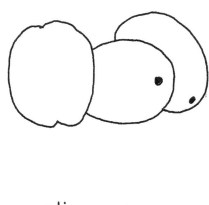

olives

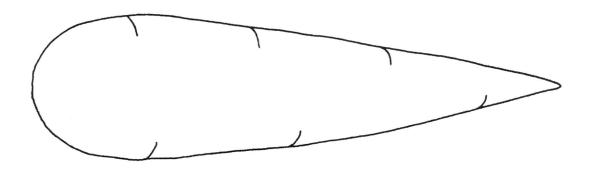

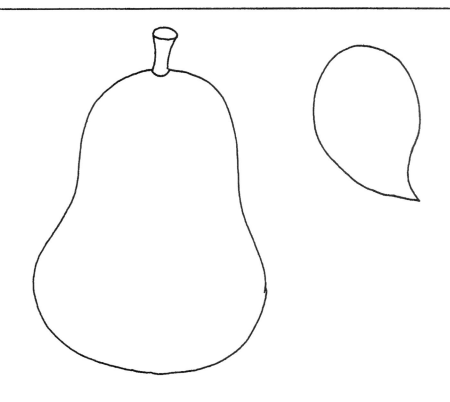

Carrot

Orange is a carrot

Yellow is a pear

Purple is a plum

And brown is a bear

Green is the grass

Blue is the sky

Black is a witch's hat

And red is cherry pie.

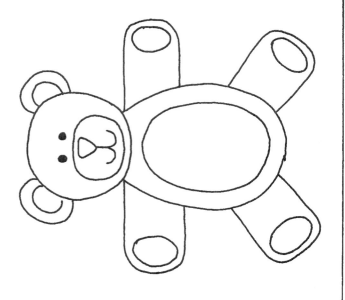

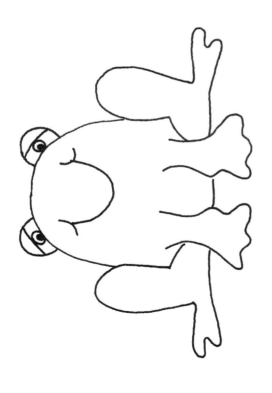

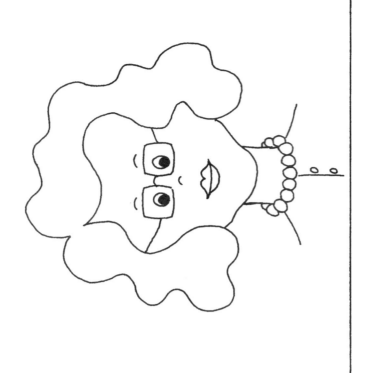

I see _____
looking at me.

Who do you see? _____

girl

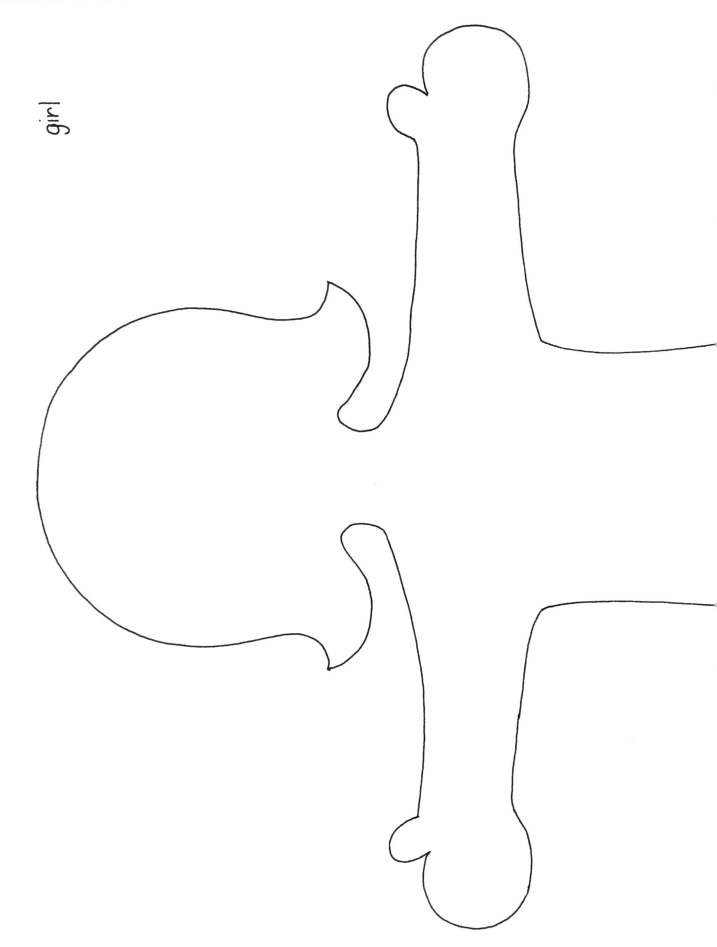

boy

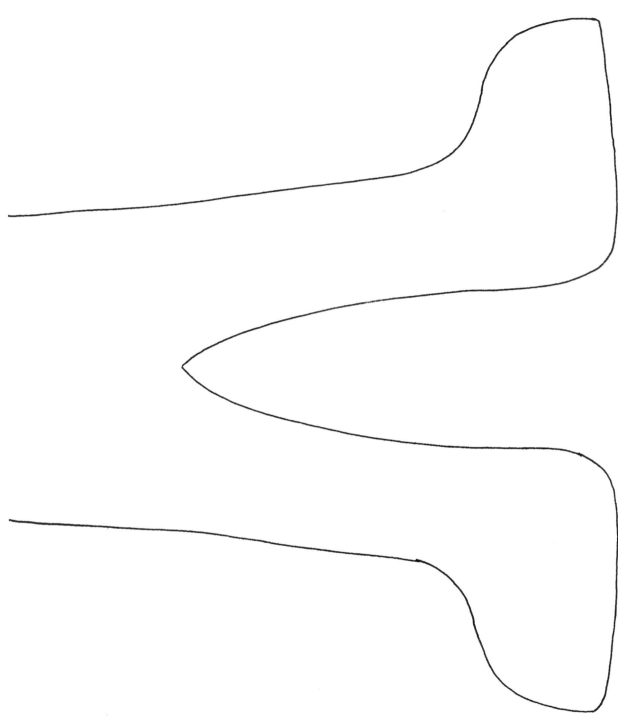

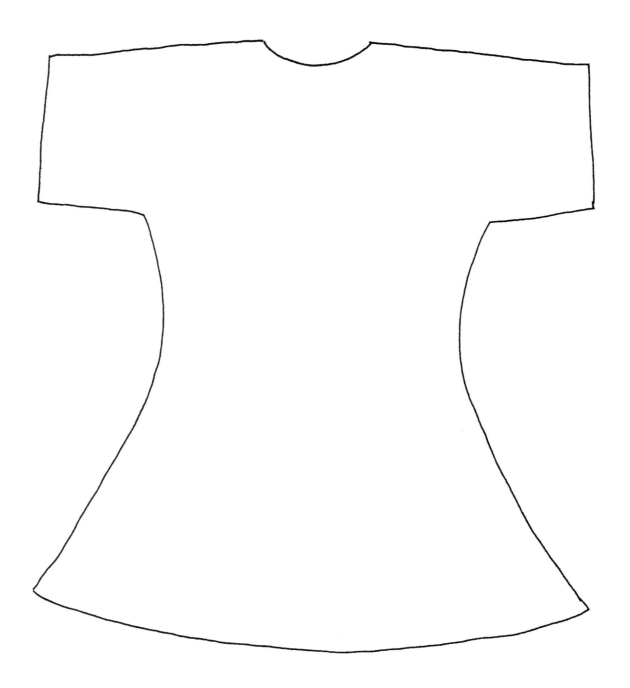

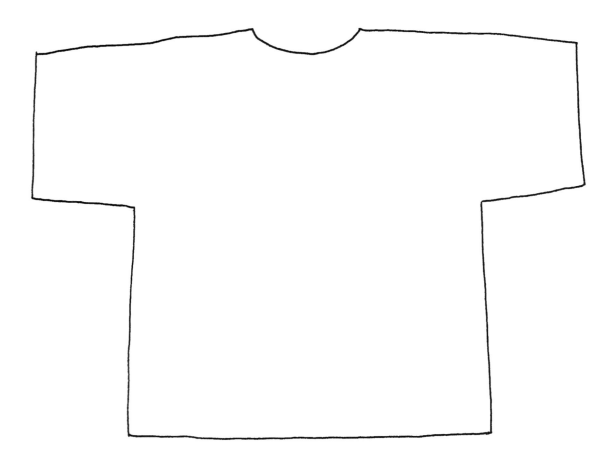

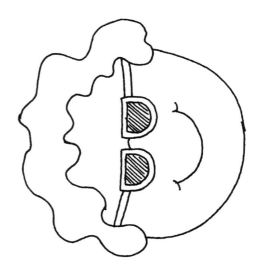

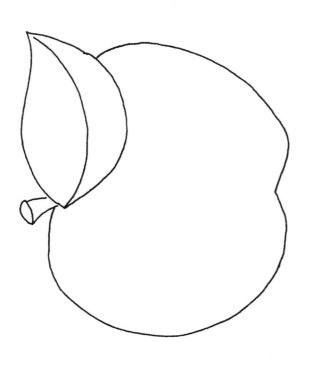

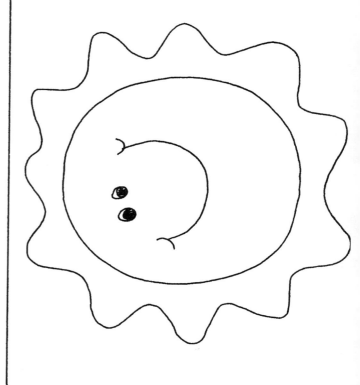

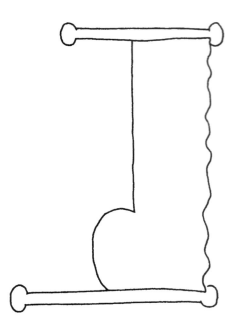

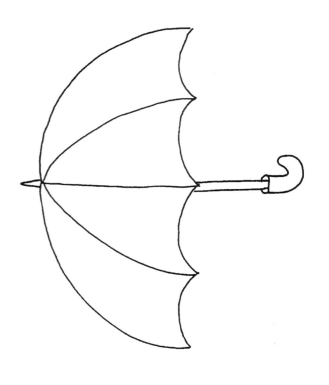

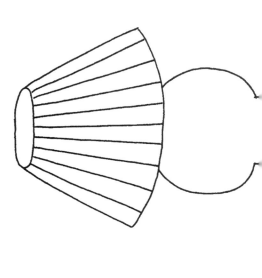

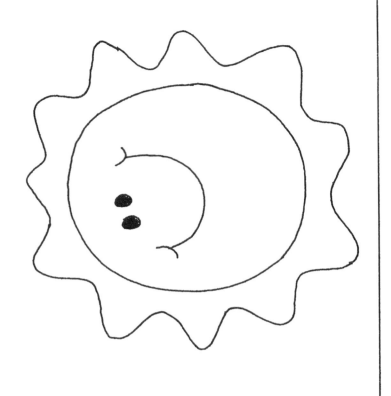

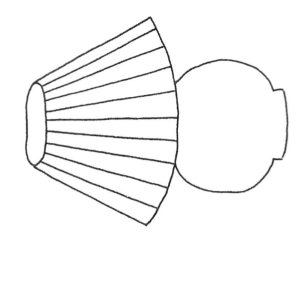

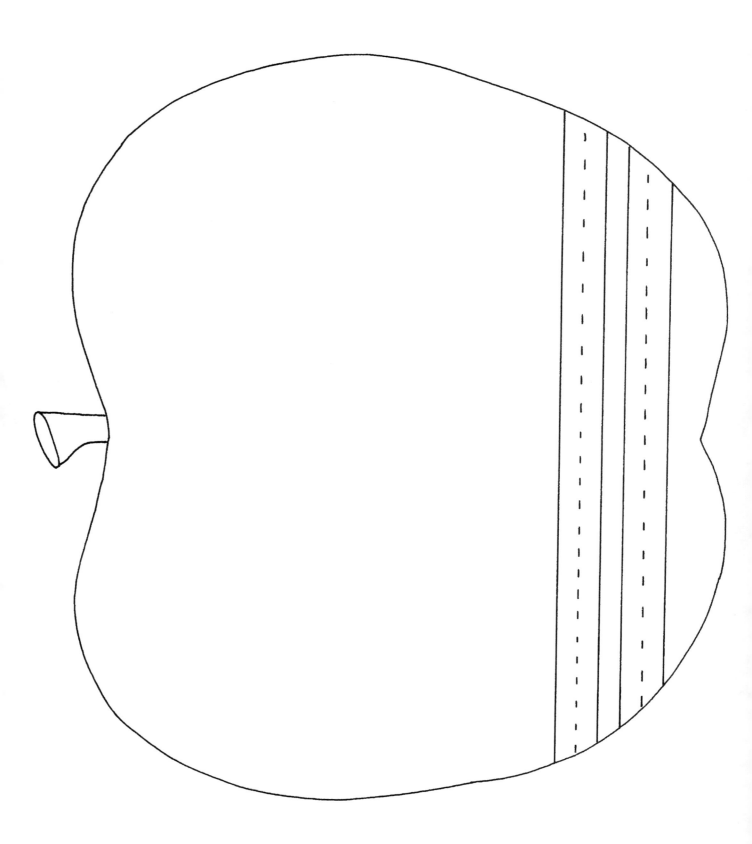

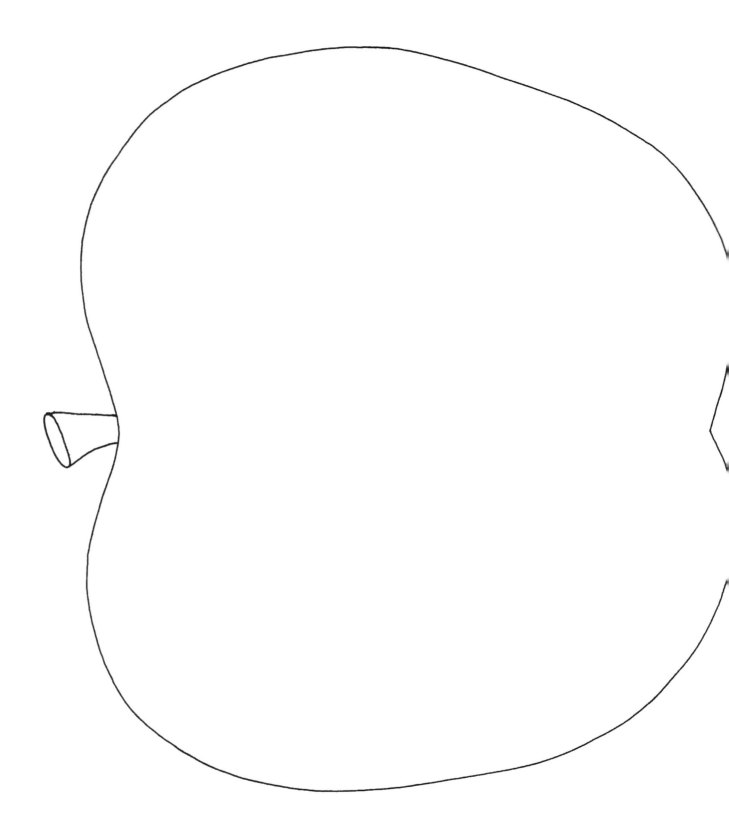

Red is an apple
on a tree

Yellow is the sun
shining on me

Orange is the umbrella
over my head

Purple is the lamp
by my bed

Green is the leaf
on a twig

Blue is the ocean
oh, so big

Grey is an elephant
I like to ride

Pink is the flower
I see outside

Brown is a rabbit
in a hat

White is white
and that is that!

The Little Red House

Once upon a time there was a little boy who was tired of all his picture books and tired of all his play.

"What shall I do?" he asked his dear mother who always knew beautiful things for little boys to do, and his dear mother said, "You shall go on a journey and find a little red house with no doors and with a star inside."

"Go down the lane and past the farmer's house and over the hill," said his dear mother. "Come back as soon as you can and tell me all about your journey."

So the little boy started out. He had not walked very far down the lane when he came to a merry little girl dancing alone in the sunshine.

"Do you know where I shall find a little red house with no doors and a star inside?" the little boy asked her.

The little girl laughed. "Ask my father, the farmer," she said.

So the little boy went on until he came to the great brown barn where the farmer himself stood in the doorway looking out over the pastures and grain fields.

"Do you know where I shall find a little red house with no doors and a star inside?" asked the little boy of the farmer.

The farmer laughed, too. "I've lived a great many years and I never saw one," he chuckled, "but ask the Granny who lives at the foot of the hill. She knows how to make arrowroot taffy and popcorn balls and red mittens. Perhaps she can direct you to it."

So the little boy went on farther still until he came to the Granny sitting in her pretty garden of herbs and marigolds.

"Please, dear Granny," asked the little boy, "Where shall I find a little red house with no doors and a star inside?"

The Granny was knitting a red mitten, but when she heard the little boy's question she laughed cheerily.

"I should like to find that little house myself," she chuckled. "It would be warm when the frosty nights come and the starlight would be prettier than a candle. But ask the wind who blows about so much and listens to all the chimneys. Perhaps the wind can direct you to the little house."

So the little boy took off his hat politely to the Granny and went on up the hill. The wind was coming down the hill as the little boy was climbing up. As they met, the wind turned about and went singing along beside him. It whistled in his ear and pushed him and dropped a pretty leaf into his hands to show what a good comrade he was.

"Oh, wind," asked the little boy after they had gone along together quite a way. "Can you help me to find a little red house with no doors and a star inside?"

The wind cannot speak in our words, but it went singing on ahead of the little boy until it came to an orchard. There it climbed up in an apple tree and shook the branches. When the little boy caught up, there at his feet lay a great, rosy apple.

The little boy picked up the apple. It was as much as his two hands could hold. It was as red as the sun had been able to paint it, and the thick brown stem stood up as straight as a chimney. It was a little red house in which the apple blossom fairly had gone to sleep.

"I wonder," thought the little boy. He took his jackknife from his pocket and cut the apple straight through the center. Oh how wonderful! There, inside the apple, lay a star holding brown seeds.

So the little boy called "Thank you!" to the wind; and the wind whistled back, "You're welcome!"

Then the little boy ran home to his mother and gave her the apple. "It is too wonderful to eat without looking at the star, isn't it?" asked the boy.

"Yes, indeed," answered his dear mother.

The Little Red House

What is

round...

and red . . .

has no windows . . .

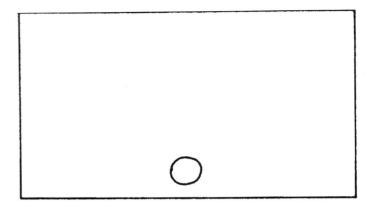

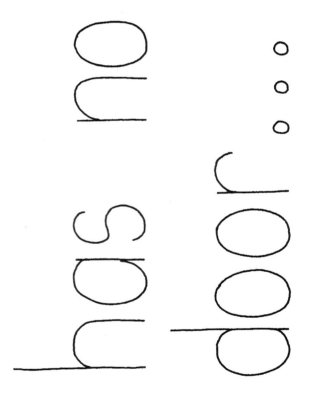

has no

door . . .

a chimney on top . . .

and a star

inside?